THE
KAMAH
SUTRAH

THE
KAMAH
SUTRAH
A BAWSTONIAN'S GUIDE TO WICKED
GOOD SEX

CIAN SMITH

CLEiS
PRESS

Published in the United States by Cleis Press, an imprint of Start Midnight, LLC, 101 Hudson Street, Thirty-Seventh Floor, Jersey City, New Jersey 07302.

Printed in the United States.
Cover design: Allyson Fields
Cover illustration: Jennifer Do, Allyson Fields
Text design: Frank Wiedemann

First Edition.
10 9 8 7 6 5 4 3 2 1

Trade paper ISBN: 978-1-62778-280-7
E-book ISBN: 978-1-62778-281-4

Library of Congress Cataloging-in-Publication Data is available on file.

For my wife: I hope ah love life will always be wicked sick.
I love you.

And for my family: thanks fur always believin' in me
and my weihd writin'. I fuckin' love ya.

DISCLAIMAH

Please always practice cawtion and be safe whenevah havin' sex or using sex toys. Some of the sex positions and sex toys in this book can seem a little outrageous, and that's because they ah, and that's because Bawstonians ah wicked crazy. You might think something is gross or unsafe, and that's probably because it is. It's a humah book. We urge you to always use ya brain and nevah do or use anything that you think might hahm you. Theah is a populah sayin' that an apple a day keeps the doctah away, but if ya choke on an apple, it can kill ya. Nawt that sex positions and toys ah like apples. I mean, I guess you could use an apple as a sex toy, but like, don't. Because that would probably hurt. Besides, wheah or how would you . . . even? Anyways, just don't take this book too seriously. Please don't sue me. I'm just a writah. I have no money.

CONTENTS

INTRODUCTION

If ya readin' this, it might be fur one of the following reasons: One, ya in a book shawp readin' the first page thinkin', *Should I even buy this very specific niche book on sex? I'm not even from Boston.* Two, ya found this book in a yahd sale next to paht one and paht two of James Cameron's mastahpiece, *Titanic,* on VHS. Three, it's the yeah 2040 and ya found this book in the rubble of what was once a book shawp and ya like, *Meh, what else am I gonna do?*

Or four, if ya really smaht, ya bawt this suckah in an attempt to open up ya sexual horizons, exploah ya innahmost sexual desiyahs, and maybe even learn a thing or two frum a wicked smaht Bawstonian such as yours truly.

If it's the last thing, then you my friend just bawt yaself an unlimited wealth of knowledge. Ya see, this is moah than just a book on sex. It's a bunch of ancient wisdom on love, relationships, and well yeah, okay, sex. It's been passed down throughout the ages of Bawston, just like Benjamin Franklin's venereal diseases.

The Kahmah Sutrah is based awff the Kama Sutra, which is an ancient Hindu text written by Vātsyāyana in Sanskrit literacha. The text is considahd to be the standahd work on human sexual behavior, and without that book ya wouldn't have this book. Ya see, the Kahmah Sutrah was written to help Bawstonians undahstand the original

Kama Sutra. We translated, interpreted, and updated the original text in ah own way, fur ah own people. Ya see, we Bawstonians are a proud bunch. We only like things frum Bawston. Anything else is weihd or different, you know, like a kid frum Maine. Ya just can't trust 'em. We Bawstonians know what we like, and what we don't like. We like ah donuts dunked, ah sox red, and ah streets to all be one-ways. You got a problem with how ah streets are all one-ways? Then leave. Ah streets ah fine! It's you who don't know how to use a GPS! But, I digress. What I'm tryin' to say is, Kahmah Sutrah was made *by* the people of Bawston *fuh* the people of Bawston. But hey, if ya nawt frum Bawston and ya wanna keep readin', be my guest! But don't get pissy when ya get none of the references, and just be happy ya didn't pick up a book about Connecticut. Gross.

What does Kahmah Sutrah even mean? Well, Kahmah translates to "wicked good sex" and Sutrah translates to "guide" or "book." In fact, this book was actually influenced by many othah books on sexual erotica specific to Bawston. One ancient text bein' *The Three Way Clover: How to Screw in Southie* by Tommy Gibbons aka Gibby the Gobbler. He got that nickname because he was the only kid in Southie that could eat a whole turkey himself on Thanksgiving. It was a sight to see fuh shoah.

Anothah text that has influenced this book is *A Mouth Full of Meatballs: How to Nob in the North End,* written by Maria Luciano. Some say she was called the Holy Mothah Mary because right aftah sex, she would make guys rise again. It was a phenomenon we Bawstonians like to call the "Res-erection."

One othah text that nawt every Bawstonian has read, but should, is *Takin' It in the Back Bay,* written by Tiffany Oldmon. It's ahnuhthah classic Bawstonian text about what and what nawt to do when havin' sex in the butt. It's a fantastic piece of literacha that covahs the subject on a whole and gets right to the point. Get it? Like . . . "whole" as in "butt hole" and "point" as in, like, "penis." You get it, you get it.

One final piece of Bawstonian sex literacha, that is more of a historic archive, is the *Politicians of Pussy,* written by the various politicians, both men and women, of Bawston. POP, fuh shawt, was a legendary group of Bawston politicians who had the gift of gab when it came to gabbing about gob. Gob, of coahse, bein' one of many Bawston slang words fuh *vagina.*

All of these historical texts passed down through the yeahs, including this book, serve as a remindah of how sex in Bawston has evolved and continues to evolve. These texts on sex ahn't just boring middle-school sex-ed lessons. They expose the true natcha of what it truly means to be frum Bawston and exploah all of ya deepest and dahkest desiyahs. We are all curious, and that's why ya got this book. It's okay to be curious. Heah, we fostah that type of thinkin' and curiosity. Imagine if you were nevah curious? Instead of Curious George, you'd just be . . . George and nobawdy likes people named George. Nawt even guys named George like people named George.

In the Kamah Sutrah, we take one step furthah and talk nawt only about sex, but also dive deep into relationships, attracting othahs to ones self, and the sex specifics in Bawston that ah different frum the rest of the world. Oh, and theah's much, much moah. We even talk about what the futcha has in stoah fuh sex, and we explain what it means to give someone a Bawston Cream Pie.

PAHT I:

SEX AS A SUBJECT

IS SEX THE ONLY THING I NEED TO BE HAPPY?

Absolutely nawt ya big dummy! Theah ah so many othah things in life that ah just as impohtant as sex. The Hindus believed that each person needed to achieve foah life goals, and Kama (desiyah) was only just one of 'em. The othah three ah Dharma, Artha, and Moksha. Dharma is to be knowledgeable in ethics, Artha in wealth, and Moksha in freedom and salvation. Howevah in Bawston, theah are only three life goals you must practice that will lead to you livin' a well-balanced life. 'Cause ya see, life is all about balance, just like ya diet. Except, with life, theah ah no cheat days. So, ya bettah fuhget about ya Weight Watchers subscription, because it ain't gonna help ya heah. You gotta get ya life in shape, and this book is gonna help to be ya fitness instructah. The three life goals fur every Bawstonian to achieve balance in ah Loyalty, Pride, and Kahmah.

Loyalty is pretty much livin' in every Bawstonian's blood frum the day they'ah boahn. If ya frum Bawston, ya bettah be Bawston Strong because if ya nawt then what ah you even? Bawston Weak?

That just sounds stupid, and I bet it doesn't look half as good on a T-shirt. Bein' loyal to ya city is just as impohtant as bein' loyal to the pahtnah ya havin' sex with, because Bawston is the only pahtnah that will nevah leave ya. Theah's gonna be times when ya wanna travel the world. Ya may even wanna move away furevah and live in New York like a Gawd damn Stahbucks-drinkin' traitah who mastahbates to Derek Jeter's fat face, or whatevah those stupid idiots do. Nevah fuhget Bawston, because Bawston nevah fuhgets you. Besides, she's had worse lovahs who have screwed her ovah. Lookin' at you Johnny "Darth Vader" Damon.

Pride is what drives the people of Bawston. We may be a smallah city, but by Gawd we make up fur it in a giant unexplained amount of confidence. We ah like a shawt guy at a bah who picks fights fuh no reason, but then buys everyone a round of drinks. That's Bawston Pride. We ah like a drunk girl on the T who throws up, but then takes a swig frum her handle of Georgi vawdka and yells at the cops that she "can do whatevah I want" because "it's my eighteenth birthday." That's Bawston Pride. We ah like a city who keeps diggin' a big hole undah the city just to make a few small changes to the highway despite financial setbacks, design flaws, and even one death. I mean that actually did happen and it was called the Big Dig, but we would do it all ovah again in a hahtbeat! Ya know why? 'Cause we ah Bawston Proud, and so should you be.

Kahmah is one life goal that Bawstonians need to talk more about. Don't get me wrong, Bawstonians love sex, but nawt all of them are educated completely on it as a subject. Whethah ya live on Beacon

Hill with the wealthiest Blue Bloods of Bawston, or ya live in sin in the city of Lynn, you should be educated on the tawpic. It's nawt just gettin' the dirt on doin' the dirty. It's about really gettin' to know yaself and ya pahtnah's ins and outs (no pun intended). Who ah you as a lovah? What ah ya interests? What ah ya desiyahs? These are all questions that ya may have nevah asked yaself because you "don't have time" and ah "just too busy." Bullshit. Make the time to get to know ya bawdy, ya mind, and ya self. I might sound like ya mothah heah, but heah me out. Ya gotta take a break frum Facebook, or Instagram, or that personal website ya creatin' to become a "professional photographah." Ya took one good pictcha of a tree without leaves in wintah with portrait mode on ya iPhone and now ya think ya Andy Warhol. Chill out. Take a break every once in a while frum everyday life so you can staht to fully enjoy ya sex life.

Don't know how to disconnect frum the preshah's of everyday life? Here ah some tips frum Bawston on how you can best cleah ya mind so that ya bawdy can be ready fuh sex.

- Light a scented candle ya bawt frum the Christmas Tree Shawp that's called Pine Tree Forest Whitaker.

- Lie on Carson Beach and have ya best bud perfoahm acupunctcha on ya with some of the used needles frum the beach.

- Meditate fuh six houahs while you wait fuh ya Megabus at South Station that's running six houahs late.

- If ya down the Cape, play a calming round of miniatcha golf at the iconic Pirate's Cove Adventure Golf in Yarmouth.

- Find a bubblah, and while the watah dribbles out, close ya eyes and pretend like ya listenin' to the crashing waves of Nantasket Beach.

- Drive by the iconic Rainbow Swash gas tank neah Intahstate 93, and breathe in the mixtcha of gas and old paint until ya high as a kite.

- If it's summah, sit at night in the Commons and listen to the calming sounds of crickets chirpin' and the distant sounds of bickering tourists who ah lawst and tryin' to find the nearest T stawp.

- If it's wintah, take a stroll right aftah a snow stoahm and listen to the beautiful crispy crunch of the freshly fallen snow undah ya boots as you carefully try to avoid stepping in dawg shit.

Some people may think that sex is a taboo subject. They'ah worried about learnin' moah because they were always taught that sex is a bad thing. But sex isn't a bad thing. You know what is a bad thing? When some sociopath fahts on a crowded T train durin' rush houah. Even a priest would condemn a psycho like that to burn in the eternal flames of hell. Sex isn't soundin' so bad now is it? If we don't educate ahselves, then we won't know how to educate ah kids and they won't know how to educate theah kids, and so on, and so on. Then we'll be stuck in a world filled with people like Jamie Lynn Spears and Casey Aldridge. No awffense to Jamie Lynn Spears; I'm a huge fan of her work.

CHAPTAH 2:

IS IT BAD TO THINK ABOUT SEX?

Ya might nawt like talkin' about sex, and that's okay. Howevah, it's crucial that ya do staht talkin' about sex, and the first step to doin' that is thinkin' about sex. It's nawt bad to think about sex. Thawts ah like spahks to a fiyah. They'll ignite ya way of communicatin' and make ya look at any subject differently. Aftah thinkin' about anything fuh too long, all you'll want to do is talk about it!

Fur example, I nevah used to shave my butt haiyah. Now, stay with me heah. I nevah used to shave my butt haiyah. But then one day I was out gettin' high with a buddy in the Commons and he asked me, "Hey, have ya evah thawt about shavin' ya butt haiyah?" And awnestly, I had nawt. I know, supah fuckin' deep question, right? It blindsided me like an oncomin' truck, and I didn't have much to say on the subject. So, I just clenched up like an unshaved butt hole and became wicked quiet. Latah that night, I couldn't stawp thinkin' about his question.

I lay awake that night thinkin' about it ovah and ovah again. I couldn't sleep. I was as curious as a cat. A cat who wanted to shave its butt haiyah. How would I do it? How would I even reach back theah? Would I need a friend? Should I ask that buddy of mine to help me shave it? So many Q's and so few A's fuh my unshaved A. I then wrote down a list of pros and cons. Pro, wipin' my butt would be easiah without haiyah catchin' all the poop. Con, in the wintah I wouldn't have tiny butt haiyahs to keep my fragile little bawttom wahwm. As ya can see, it was a conundrum, but I was ready to talk about it with someone.

The next week, I was out with that same buddy. We were gettin' high in the Bawston Public Gardens, and my buddy asked me the same question as befoah. At first I was like, "Do ya evah think about anythin' else besides shavin' ya butt?" And he was like, "Awnestly, nah. It's all I evah think about." I apologized to him and told him that he wasn't alone. I confessed that evah since he asked me, I too had been thinkin' about it non stawp. That night we made a pact. We decided that we would both shave ah butts, and then meet up the next day to see how we liked it. We both walked out of those gahdens that night as changed men. The next day, we both agreed that shavin' ah butts was the best decision we have evah made in our entiyah lives. Since then, my butt has been as bald as a bowling ball. Coincidentally enough, it also has three holes due to a run-in with a rhinoceros one time at Franklin Park Zoo, but I digress. What I'm tryin' to get at is that it's impohtant fur everyone to first *think* about sex, so they can then finally staht talkin' about it.

Some people are okay with talkin' about sex, but when it comes to havin' sex they have all these excuses as to why they can't do it.

"I'm too busy with work," "I can't find the right person," "I'm a priest." Okay, well the priest thing makes sense, and with this bein' a book about sex frum Bawston, let's just stay away frum Priests altogethah. Heah are a bunch of excuses that most people frum Bawston, and around the world, use to avoid havin' sex.

"I'm a practicin' Catholic. I don't think it is okay fuh me to enjoy sex." What ah you talkin' about, ya dummy! Gawd practically wants ya to have sex and repawpulate the Earth with tons of little ones. Yeah, maybe he wants ya to wait 'til marriage, but who cares? He ain't gonna be mad if ya bring some moah little cryin' baby Catholics into his church on Eastah and Christmas.

"I work long houahs, and I don't have time fuh sex." But ya got time to read a book about sex? Put down this book right now, go have sex, and then come back to continue readin' how you can be havin' sex bettah.

"I don't have a pahtnah, and I don't wanna have a one-night stand." Stawp fuckin' around and get on some datin' apps so you can get to go on some dates, meet someone ya feel comfuhtable with, and then get to fuckin' around.

"I'm afraid of havin' sex 'cause I don't wanna get pregnant." Theah's an old sayin' that is the same in any lan-

guage and that rings true all the way frum Bawston to Bolivia: "Don't be a fool, wrap ya tool."

"The last time I had sex was when the Red Sox won the 2004 World Series, and I'm afraid that it will nevah feel the same again as it did on that magical night." Awnestly, you are absolutely right. It will nevah be as good as it was that night, but ya can't let that get in the way of you havin' sex. It's just somethin' ya gonna have to learn to live with.

"I can't find the right person to have sex with." Be patient, take ya time, but make shoah ya don't set ya standahds too high. Just remembah, no one is perfect. Well, except fuh Beyoncé, but she's already taken.

"I can't have sex because I have sexually transmitted infections." You should check with ya doctah to see what protection you can get and how you can still have sex. Just don't go tryin' to fix it through WebMD. No mattah how much ya love *Grey's Anatomy*, you ah nawt and will nevah be a real doctah.

"I don't wanna have sex because I'm afraid I'll be too loud and my neighbahs will heah me." Then play some heavy metal music or crank up a fight scene frum any of

the *Transformers* movies. When ya neighbahs complain about the loud noises, just be like, "It's eithah that or me havin' sex." And ya neighbahs will be like, "Just have the loud sex! Fuh the love of Gawd, that would be so much bettah than Metallica at two in the morning."

"I have too many errands and don't have time to think about sex, let alone have it." Ya nawt a protagonist of a Lifetime Original Movie. Ya gotta make some time fur it. It's unhealthy if ya only evah goin' frum home, to work, to CVS, to the bank, to grocery shawppin', and then back home every single day.

"I can nevah get in the mood to have sex because I need it to be completely quiet, and I live right next to the T train tracks." Well then move!

"I hate havin' sex because durin' the act of havin' sex, I faht out my poop chute." What the hell? That's disgusting. Go see a doctah fuh Christ's sake!

"My bed is covahd with Beanie Babies so theah's no room fuh sex." They may be a collectah's item, but they can always be moved to ahnuhthah paht of ya house, ya psycho.

"I don't like sex, and I think it's yucky." Then why ah you reading this book?

"I simply don't know how to have sex." Did you nawt have sex-ed as a kid? Regahdless, theah ah many videos on the World Wide Web that will give you some insight on how it's done. Just don't go too fah down that rabbit hole because then you'll staht seein' stuff with actual rabbits.

"All my ex-girlfriends say I gotta wicked big dick, so I don't wanna have sex because I'm afraid I'm gonna hurt someone." LOL, yah right, go fuck yaself.

DOES THIS MEAN I HAVE TO HAVE SEX ALL THE TIME?

Look, no one is tellin' ya that ya gotta have sex all the time, twenty-foah/seven, nonstawp bing-bang-boom-in-the-room. Sex is all about balance. If you don't have enough of it, ya can become like Whitey Bulger. You'll staht feelin' angry at life and like ya wanna kill everyone. If ya have too much sex, ya could also become like Whitey Bulger. You'll staht feelin' easily bored with it all and will staht killin' people outta apathy. Well both of those examples might be a stretch, but what I guess I'm tryin' to say is, just don't be like Whitey Bulger.

The lesson heah is that sex is best in moderation. When you have too much sex, it can sometimes lose its magic. Imagine goin' to Disney World every day fuh like a week straight. Shoah you'd have a blast, and Space Mountain would always be the most fun you've evah had in ya life. But, by like the fifth day of the week ya like, "All right, I've done all the fun rides . . . I guess, now I'll go on Walt Disney's Carousel of Progress?" On the flip side, when ya don't have enough sex, you might go crazy or get carpal tunnel in the wrist.

Theah may come a time when you and ya pahtnah need a break frum sex, and that is totally natural. You might be sick. You might be tiyahd. You might still have bruises frum the time you tried to have sex on ya brand new kitchen table and the table collapsed. You can use this break frum sex as a way to build up the anticipation in the bedroom. Nawt shoah what to do besides have sex? Well, when you'ah nawt on the phone to ya Bernie and Phyl's representative tryin' to explain how ya kitchen table just broke and why theah are ass cheek mahks on it, heah ah some ways to pass the time.

- Make a sandwich.
- Read a book.
- Do laundry.
- Play a cahd game. Like the evah-so-populah Go Fish.
- Sit on a couch and think about life and how we'ah all gonna die someday.
- Fly a kite (if theah is wind outside).
- Staple some pieces of papah togethah.
- Organize the pens in the pen holdah on ya desk.
- Go fur a walk.
- Pet a dawg.
- Go to Bed Bath and Beyond.

- Collect stamps.
- Feed a bird.
- Untie a knawt.
- Sit on a pahk bench and contemplate ya existence and why you ah heah on Earth.
- Knit a hat.
- Finish a puzzle.
- Light a new Yankee Candle ya got frum the Christmas Tree Shawp.
- Eat the sandwich you made frum earliyah.
- Lie awake in bed at night, at three in the mornin', thinkin' about how we'ah only tiny bawlls of energy existing in a universe that is paht of a multiverse.
- Wash ya dishes.

WHAT TYPE OF PEOPLE SHOULD I HAVE SEX WITH?

You sometimes may want a roll in the hay with a strangah that you only just met that day. Although these words may be true, and may also sound like somethin' out of a Dr. Seuss book, sex with the right person is very impohtant. Now, frum time to time, ya may want to go slummin' in the streets fur a freak in the sheets, but if ya gonna do that in Bawston ya gotta be smaht about it. Shoah, sex is way bettah with someone ya love, but every single man and woman of Bawston can agree that sometimes, fuh the lack of a bettah phrase, ya just gotta get it in.

Full dislaimah heah, theah ah people that you should have sex with and people you should absolutely nevah have sex with in Bawston. So befoah you go deep sea fishin' out in the big ocean of Bawstonians, heah ah some helpful tips to make shoah you end up with a lovable creatcha like the one in *Shape of Water* and nawt like the one in *Creature from the Black Lagoon*.

Now, you may disagree with these lists, but these lists have been carefully crafted ovah many yeahs. Some people that ah good to have sex with include:

- Any girl or guy who can name all the playahs' names on the Red Sox.
- Any girl or guy who can name all the playahs' names on the Bruins.
- Any girl or guy who can name all the playahs' names on the Patriots.
- Any girl or guy who can name all the playahs' names on the Celtics.
- Any girl or guy who buys you Philips Candy House chocolates fur any reason evah.
- Guys that play Beatles, AC/DC, or Buddy King on the electric guitar.
- Girls that can play the drums, bass, or piano.
- Girls that go to Boston University, Emerson, or Boston College.
- Guys that go to MIT, Northeastern, or Berekley.
- Any girl or guy who works at Boston Children's Hospital.
- Any girl or guy that gets a high scoah on a game at Dave & Buster's.

- Any girl or guy that is proud of the rich American history in the great city of Bawston.

- Any girl or guy that loves goin' to Water Wizz, Water Country, and/or Six Flags: New England.

- Any girl or guy who loves to watch *Family Guy*.

- Any girl or guy that has Verizon or AT&T.

- Any girl or guy that has an iPhone or Samsung phone.

- Any girl or guy that was actually boahn in the city of Bawston.

Heah ah some people that you should absolutely nevah have sex with undah any circumstances evah. Nawt even once.

- Guys that play Goo Goo Dolls, Dave Matthews Band, or Dispatch on the acoustic guitah.

- Guys that go to Harvard.

- Girls that go to UMass.

- Guys that weah Sperrys in the wintah.

- Girls that weah Ugg boots in the summah.

- Any girl or guy that has T-Mobile or Sprint.

- Any girl or guy that has a Motorola or an HTC phone.

- Any girl or guy that weahs a Red Sox, Bruins, Patriots, or Celtics hat but can't name one single player on the team.

- Any girl or guy that is frum western Massachusetts but pretends to have a Bawston accent.

- Any girl or guy frum Rhode Island that pretends to know more about the Red Sox than you.

- Any girl or guy that hates goin' to the Cape in the summah.

- Any girl or guy that hates eatin' lobstah.

- Any girl or guy that talks durin' a movie in the AMC Loews at the Commons.

- Any girl or guy that loves to watch *The Big Bang Theory*.

- Any drunk girl named Tiffany.

- Any drunk guy named Paul.

- Drunk girls or guys that sing Taylor Swift at karaoke.

- Guys that do stand up at Dick Doherty's Beantown Comedy Club.

- Guys named Derrick who work the Duck Tours.

- Any girl or guy who pukes in the middle of Yawkey Way.

- Any guy that works at Lids at the South Shore Plaza.

- Any girl that works at Olive Garden at Patriot Place.

- Any guy or girl who likes the Yankees.

- Literally any girl named Crystal. The only Crystal you should evah have is the Waterford one that ya Irish grandmothah left ya when she died.

HOW DO I KNOW IF IT'S TIME FUH SEX?

Befoah sex, you and ya pahtnah must one-hundred-puhcent agree that you would both like to have sex with one ahnuhthah. Consent is paramount. If one of you isn't feelin' in the mood, or doesn't want to have sex, then ya can't have sex. Durin' sex, you both also must be one-hundred-puhcent onboahd with the type of sex ya wanna have. Ya gotta communicate, and if theah is somethin' you or ya pahtnah doesn't feel comfuhtable doin', then ya can't do it. It's as simple as that. Theah is no gray area.

I'll give you an example frum my own personal life. When my wife says we'ah nawt havin' sex, I know I have no othah choice than to go to the kitchen and make myself a peanut buttah and fluff sandwich and remembah that theah are othah things in life that come pretty close to sex, and that's one of them. Now, if you have nevah had a peanut buttah and fluff sandwich, I am so sorry to say that you nevah had a real childhood. Your childhood was a fake and a sham and did nawt exist. If you have had peanut buttah and fluff sandwiches and you don't like them, I am so sorry to say that I do nawt like you. We will nevah be friends.

Sex is a lawt like dancing, just moah . . . horizontal. So, let's use dancing in an analogy fuh sexual consent. Even bettah, because theah are a ton of Irish people in Bawston, let's equate consensual sex to Irish step dancing.

If you ask someone, "Would you like to do a jig?" and they say "No," then they do nawt wanna Irish step dance with you. They might nawt be in the mood to jig, or they might just nawt feel comfuhtable dancing a jig because you just met, or they might nawt think you ah the best pahtnah to have a jig with. Now, this doesn't mean they hate Irish step dancing. Maybe they've even taken paht in a jig or two in the back room of Florian Hall at a nice Irish wedding. The point is, if they don't feel like doin' a jig at that present time, then you can't force them to do a jig. Jigs ah fun and happy and lighthearted, and no one wants to be forced to do one. Also, you can't make someone jig if they don't want to, because that would requiah you to physically move theah bawdy around and no one wants that.

Let's say you see someone tapping theah foot to the lovely lilt of an Irish tune by the Wolf Tones. If you go up and say, "Hey, I see you tapping ya foot, would you like to do a jig?" and they say, "No, I'm okay, thank you," then that means they do nawt wanna do a jig. You could say, "But I saw you tapping ya foot. You ah practically asking to do a jig!" And they might say, "Well, sometimes I just like to tap my foot because I enjoy a nice Irish tune, but that doesn't mean I want to do a jig." Even though it looked like they might want to do a jig, it's been made cleah to you that they do nawt wanna do a jig with you. That means you can't do a jig with them.

Now, sometimes tapping a foot *can* lead to doin' a jig, but again, even if someone taps theah foot, it doesn't mean you can do a jig with them if they don't want to. If that same person who was tapping theah foot takes paht in a jig with someone else, you cannawt get mad at them fuh dancing with someone else. Also, you absolutely cannawt go ovah and break up theah dancing and staht doin' a jig with that person who didn't wanna dance with you befoah. It's a very rude thing to do, and you'll also probably get a punch to the face.

You might find yaself on a date with someone, and you might find yaself stumbling into a bah togethah. Let's say ya both a bit tipsy, and you've been talkin' about doin' a jig all night—you even did a couple of trebles and clicks in the hallway back neah the bathrooms. If the time finally comes to do a jig, and the othah person says, "Hey, I don't feel like doin' a jig anymoah," then that means they do nawt wanna do a jig. And what's impohtant to remembah is: they don't have to. Even though you had talked about dancing all night, and how excited you were to do a jig, you cannawt do a jig with them. You might say, "It's okay, we don't have do a jig, we can just do a quick reel." But if the person says, "No thanks," that means they don't want to dance at all. They don't wanna do a reel, a jig, or even a slip jig, weah it's a quick in-and-out routine. They just do nawt wanna do any dancing, and that means you can't dance. The best thing to do then, if you still feel like dancin', is to go home and watch *Riverdance* and do a hornpipe by yaself.

If you ask someone, "Hey, would you like to do a jig?" and they don't respond, then—and I think this should go without sayin' by now—DO NAWT do a jig with them. They might be either asleep, passed out, or unresponsive, and if any of those ah the case, then absolutely undah no circumstances, evah, should you try to do a jig with them. Also, if they ah unresponsive, you should be thinkin' about calling the police fuh help, nawt thinkin' about tryin' to dance with them.

If you ask someone, "Would you like to do a jig?" and they respond, "Yes, I would love to do a jig with you!" then you should go and enjoy a nice jig! Durin' the dancing, if the person stawps and says, "You know what, I actually don't feel like doin' a jig anymoah," then stawp dancing. But if you staht to do a jig, and the othah person is all like, "Oh my Gawd this is the best jig evahhhhhhhh. Don't stawp! Don't stawp!" then you fuckin' jig the shit out of that dance floah togethah like you ah the Gawd damn lords of the dance.

SEX AS A PRACTICE

WHAT DO I DO WITH MY JUNK?

It may come as a surprise to ya if ya nevah been in a showah or lockah room with ahnuhthah person of the same sex, but theah ah tons of people out theah with all different shapes and sizes of junk. That's right, big junk, little junk, fat junk, skinny junk, and junk that would make ya look at it and go, "Whoah! What is that? I've nevah even seen something like that befoah! I wanna get to know it. I wanna become friends with it. Get me a night on the town and a table fuh two at Del Frisco's with that junk!" We live in a land of junk that is all different and unique and that's what makes this country so great. You might even have junk that's a little funky lookin' and in Bawston we call that "funk junk."

If you think you have "funk junk," and ya down in the dumps about it, ya gotta realize that it is a good thing. When it comes to ya junk, ya gotta be proud of its individuality. It might look like ya got a bowl of fruit that got in a juicing accident, but at the end of the day ya gotta accept ya bawdy and be happy with it because it's the only one ya got. Also, more impohtantly, make shoah the person ya havin' sex with loves ya bawdy just as much as you do. Don't go changin' ya bawdy just because someone says you should. If you think you want to make changes to ya bawdy, it should always be your own decision. Always treat ya bawdy like a temple. And don't just go to any old doc-tah to get work done. Trust me, theah ah some wicked shady doctahs in Lynn that'll promise ya a boob lift fur a thousand bucks and a ham sandwich. It doesn't even have to be good ham. Like, it could be a cold cut frum 7-Eleven fur all they care.

We gotta embrace ah differences. Imagine a world full of people who all looked the same and had the same lookin' junk. That would be terrible! We would all be like a bunch of plastic Barbie and Ken dolls. Nawt to mention, Barbie doesn't have a vagina and Ken doesn't have a penis, so like what the fuck is that shit? No one wants that. Unless you do, then again theah ah places in Lynn fuh that sort of thing.

You may have a tiny dick, and that's okay! You may have a wide vagina, and that's okay too! What ya gotta know about ya junk is that it's like a puzzle piece. Every piece has a countahpaht that fits it perfectly. If ya evah feel like a lawst piece of a puzzle, be patient because sometimes it takes a while to find the right fit. But enough about puzzles. Puzzles suck. They ah wicked confusing and always make ya head hurt. Instead of puzzles, we Bawstonians use populah architectcha of Bawston to explain what types and different sizes of junk are out theah in the world. We do this mostly because build-ings ah like biggah shapes, and biggah shapes ah wicked cool to look at and easiah to undahstand.

But hold on, we'ah gettin' way ahead of ahselves. Befoah we staht talkin' about different shapes of penises and vaginas, we first gotta go ovah the slang words Bawstonians use to refah to penises and vaginas. Some slang words you may have heard used around the world might be: cock, Johnson, pussy, dick, clam, vertical smile, purple helmet soldiah, beef curtains—you get the pictcha. So, why do Bawstonians have specific slang words fuh sex pahts, when so many already exist? Because, we ah frum Bawston, and we like to do things ah own way. You evah see us drive? We use the breakdown lane as just ahnuhthah lane to drive in. You know why? Because, we decided it. It's an unspoken rule that we all live by, and if you don't like ah rules, then leave. Also, get out of ah way because if you ah in the breakdown lane, we will hit you and we will drive away.

We only have one name fur a penis in Bawston and it's called a Fenway Frank. We only have one name fur a vagina in Bawston and it's called a Dunkin' Donut. We call testicles Munchkins, and we call a clitoris a Sprinkle. We name all ah sex pahts aftah these favorite Bawston foods because they ah guilty pleashas. Just don't try to have sex with an actual Fenway Frank or Dunkin' Donut even though the real things ah pretty tempting.

Now, back to the architectcha of Bawston and how it relates to different sizes of junk. Fuh guys, we have broken it down to three different sizes of The Frank and they are: a Hancock, a State, and a Revere.

A Hancock is named aftah the John Hancock Tower, one of the biggest buildings in Bawston. A Hancock is a guy who usually can't weah tightfitting pants, but if he's confident he'll do it anyway. A Hancock is a guy that when ya ask him, "How's it hangin'?" he'll usually respond with, "Long." A Hancock rarely evah gets into fights because he knows he doesn't have to with a Frank that big. Although he's got a big head, he's usually good about thinkin' with his brain instead of his head. A Hancock is a sight to see, and many women frum around the world ah very impressed with its size in a city that doesn't have many skyscrapers. It's rumahed that even John Hancock himself had a huge Frank. Why else do ya think he had a big signatcha on the Declaration of Independance?

A State is named aftah the State House, a building that is admired by many Bawstonians, but isn't the biggest building you've evah seen. A State is a guy usually with a nice dome piece, but relatively average in size. A guy who is a State usually wishes he was a Hancock, but he's just happy he's nawt a Revere. A State is a guy that, like the building, is really beautiful inside, like as a person, but on the outside he kind of blends in with all the othah guys. Nawt to say that the State House is nawt beautiful on the outside, but it usually gets looked ovah and taken fuh granted. A guy who is a State is the type of guy who dates a couple of girls, but then ends up marrying his high school or cawllege sweetheart, He's the type of guy ya bring home to ya parents, and ya dad likes because he doesn't feel intimidated.

A Revere is named aftah Paul Revere's House located in the North End of Bawston. When it was first built, it was considahd a pretty big house, but compahed to the buildings of today it comes up shawt. A guy who is a Revere is always stahtin' fights or drivin' flashy cahs. It was rumahed that Paul Revere also had a small Frank. It explains why he pretty much took all the credit fuh the Midnight Ride. A guy who is a Revere usually tries to get people to look at it every day and is afraid of gettin' lawst in the shuffle. In some ways, it's almost a sight to see, nawt because it's historic like Paul Revere's actual house, but because it's so small. We also call these men a Revere, because we revere them fuh havin such tiny Franks. It's nawt an easy thing to live with, and these men ah true patriots fightin' the good fight. They'ah just tryin to live theah best, tiny Frank lives so leave 'em alone.

Fuh women, theah ah three different types of Donuts, and they are: a Big Dig, a Pavilion, and a Fenway.

A Big Dig is named aftah, of coahse, the Big Dig. It describes a woman who is biggah in size. A Big Dig is a woman who can allow a lot of traffic inside her; she's built to handle wide loads and can fit some pretty big trucks. Rumah has it, Ted Williams was a lovah of Big Digs, so much so that one of the tunnels in the Big Dig was named aftah him. Ahnuhthah rumah was that Ted Williams earned the name "The Greatest Hittah Who Ever Lived" nawt only because of his amazing baseball career, but because of his ability to scoah with tons of women who were Big Digs. We like to believe that ol' Teddy "The Thumper" Williams is up in Heaven smilin' down, knowin' that theah is a tunnel named aftah him that runs through the Big Dig furevah. Now, of coahse, the actual Big Dig project was an absolute nightmah and cawst millions of dollahs, but a woman who is a Big

Dig should nawt be held accountable fuh that. She is an absolute treasha to behold and can hold you safely within her open Donut.

A Pavilion is named aftah the Pavilion amphitheater. It's usually a woman who is lahge, but nawt like wicked huge in size. A Pavilion can fit a lawt of people but is selective of who she lets in because she is nawt as big as a Big Dig. A woman who is a Pavilion is always gonna be a good time, because theah is always a really good show that you've been dyin' to see inside. Because of its size, it sometimes can get ovah crowded and people spill theah beeah all ovah the place, makin' it kind of easy to get wet. A Pavilion is nawt always open to the public, but will always open its dooahs fuh a rock 'n' roll band or a hip hop musician. Howevah, frum time to time, a Pavilion will make a bad decision and have an ahtist like STAIND perfoahm inside, and it turns awff a lawt of people. That's somethin' that is just real tough to nawt think about when ya havin' sex with a Pavilion.

A Fenway is named aftah none othah than the very home away frum home, Fenway Park. Every Bawstonian loves a Fenway. A woman who is a Fenway is smallah in size, which is true to the actual Fenway Park because it's more intimate than most othah ballpahks. It's a place that ya love to go to, and everytime ya go it feels like the very first time. A Frank would be lucky to be found inside a Fenway but can only get theah frum time to time because it's nawt always open. The hedges are always trimmed, and inside theah is a Pink Monstah and when ya hit that spawt, it feels like an absolute home run. Because of her size, a Fenway has to be very selective of who she lets inside. A Fenway can sometimes be cruel to you. She can tease you, and torment you fuh many yeahs. We know that has nothin' to do with size but, regahdless, it's just a known thing in Bawston that you will always experience the highest highs and the lowest lows with a Fenway. But no mattah how much she teases you, fuh some reason, you always find ya self goin' back fuh moah.

Now that you have an undahstanding of how Bawstonians talk about the different sizes of Franks and Donuts, you can undahstand how they fit togethah. Certain sizes ah moah compatible with one ahnuhthah than othahs, and it's impohtant to know that to increase ya sexual pleasha.

A Hancock fits perfectly with a woman who is a Big Dig, fits amazing with a woman who is a Pavilion, but is too big fur a woman who is a Fenway.

A State fits okay with a woman who is a Big Dig, fits perfectly with a woman who is a Pavilion, and fits amazing with a woman who is a Fenway.

A Revere does nawt fit a woman who is a Big Dig at all, fits okay with a woman who is a Pavilion, and fits perfectly with a woman who is a Fenway.

Of coahse, you can always try to mix it up and push the boundaries when it comes to these different sizes and combinations. Don't get discouraged if it doesn't work out. As much as every Bawstonian guy would love to fit the entiyah Hancock building into Fenway Park, it just isn't gonna happen. It's like watchin' a toddlah tryin' to slam a triangle block through a circulah hole in his play set. It's the most adorable thing you evah saw, but it's very messy and looks painful fuh everyone involved.

It's best to know what type of Bawston architectcha you are, and how you fit into the rest of the city and its residents. You may have nevah given any thawt to it befoah but knowing this is the first step to increasing sexual pleasha in the bedroom. This is also proof that no mattah the size of ya junk, theah is someone out theah that is a perfect fit just fuh you.

HOW DO I KISS GOOD?

If you have evah had sex befoah, then you probably already know how to kiss. Howevah, chances ah you could have been doin' it wrong this entiyah time! Scary stuff, right? It's as if you were Bruce Willis at the end of *Sixth Sense* and ya findin' out you were dead the whole time. Remembah that movie? Oh my Gawd, what a sick movie. If you have nevah seen that movie, go see that movie! That scene, when Bruce finds out he was dead the whole time, is such an amazing scene to experience fuh the first time. Ya see, Bruce Willis is shawt in the beginnin' of the movie, but then they just kinda, like, continue the movie and don't really address it. But then, like, Bruce meets this kid, and the kid claims that he can see dead people, and then at the end of the movie Bruce realizes that he's one of the dead people that the kid's been seein'! Such a wicked good movie. Ya gotta go see it.

Anyways, kissin' is like the best thing to staht with befoah sex because it's a foahm of foahplay. It gets ya excited and, if ya do it right, it can stimulate ya sex drive. Bawstonians love kissin', especially the

Irish Bawstonians. Why do ya think they're always askin' everyone to kiss them on St. Paddy's Day? They even kiss stones, the crazy sons of bitches. If ya need to know how to kiss bettah, heah is how ya do it.

Tilt ya head to one side, but just make shoah that ya don't tilt it the same way as the person kissin' ya, cuz then you'll just look like a bunch of turkeys who know nothin' about anything. Lean in, slowly, and hold the person by theah waist or shouldahs if they'ah tall. Open ya mouth, but nawt too wide because then you'll look like ya yawnin' or givin' an invisible giant a blow job. Move in closah, and then press ya lips softly against the othah person's lips. Move ya lips up and down and all around as if ya chewin' bubble gum, but like small Chiclet bubble gum and nawt Hubba Bubba. It's kinda like takin' a sip frum a nice cool bubblah on a hawt summah's day. Think of that watah hittin' ya lips and you just drinkin' it all up. Paints a pretty pictcha fuh ya, huh? Just don't be kissin' anyone with them dry lips. If you do find ol' Charlie Chap Lips, you give 'em a dollah and a coupon to CVS and say, "The ChapStick is on me."

Once ya feel like you've mastahd the aht of kissin' and ya lips ah feelin' wettah than LL Cool J's (why is he always lickin' his lips?), you can move on to more advanced versions of kissin'. Once ya gently insert ya tongue into the othah person's mouth, ya gonna wanna move it around like a fish that flopped on a deck. But just don't be, like, violent about it. You'll want to staht movin' ya tongue up and down and all around, gently massagin' the othah person's tongue. Think of it like ya lickin' stamps, but instead of that yucky envelope glue taste, you'll get a mouth full of thick, wet, tongue. Okay, it sounds gross written out like this, but trust me it's totally worth it. Again, be gentle. No one likes gettin' a tongue jammed down theah throat like theah larynx is bein' checked fuh swollen lymph nodes.

Some things ya nevah gonna wanna do while kissin' ah the followin':

- Eat food.
- Cough.
- Sneeze.
- Chew bubble gum.
- Yawn.
- Suck in aiyah.
- Try to get food out of ya teeth.
- Beat bawx.
- Make faht noises with ya mouth as a joke.
- Sing.
- Stick ya tongue out.
- Scream.
- Talk about how much you love the scene frum *Sixth Sense* when Bruce Willis's charactah realizes he's been dead the whole time.
- Whistle.

Ya really can't go wrong, so long as you don't do these things while kissin', and ya follow those previously laid out directions on how to kiss good. At the end of the day, it's all about havin' the right amount of confidence. It's okay to try and fail, but if ya gonna talk a big game and tell everyone how good you are as a kissah, you bettah be able to live up to that reputation. You gotta be ready to put ya money wheah ya mouth is, except don't actually put money in ya mouth because that is disgusting, and no one is gonna wanna kiss ya.

CHAPTAH 8:

SHOULD I DO FOAHPLAY?

Kissin' is like the softest foahm of foahplay, and trust me, ya gonna wanna do much moah than kissin' to get the othah person excited and in the mood. Especially if you've been havin' sex with the same person fur a very long time. Things can get stale and boring, and that's nawt ya fault. Once ya staht blamin' yaself or ya pahtnah fuh sex feelin' like a routine, then ya gonna go down a dahk and slippery slope. It's nawt gonna be like a fun, dahk, and slippery slope like an excited woman's Donut. It's gonna be a scary, dahk, and slippery slope like in *The Goonies* when they all fell into that tunnel undahneath that abandoned restaurant.

The key to foahplay is knowin' that it takes time. You might always wanna get straight to makin' the sex, but it doesn't work like that. Foahplay is a must fur a lot of pahtnahs, no mattah theah gendah. So, you got some work to do befoah you staht slidin' into home. First, ya gotta round the bases.

Sex can feel like a choah sometimes, especially when it's cold outside. Ya gotta get undressed, but then it's cold, so ya gotta hop undah the sheets, but then the sheets ah wahwm, so then ya get sleepy—it's a whole thing. No mattah what, ya gotta always remembah that sex can sometimes feel like work and that's okay! Once you accept that way of thinkin' you ah ready to open ya mind and bawdy to ya pahtnah. In Bawston, theah ah three exciting ways to practice good foahplay: light scratching, sucking of the neck, and light biting. Coincidentally enough, these are also three things that pain-in-the-ass bugs do to ya when ya on the beach down the Cape.

When you wanna practice some light scratching, the best method of exciting ya pahtnah is to take ya nails and lightly scratch the route of the Bawston Marathon in theah back. You have ya pahtnah lie on theah stomach, and if you want to add to the scratching you can even role-play. You can wispah things in theah eah like, "Hey baby, wanna go fur a run?" or "I can't wait to go the distance with you," or "I'm gonna fuck you so good, but befoah that, I'm gonna scratch the entiyah route of the Bawston Marthon into ya back."

Staht at the small of theah back, pretending like it's Hopkinton, and then take them on a run. Brush ya fingah up through Ashland, and Framingham, and then around the centah of theah back like you'ah just comin' up to Natick. Now, once ya get to Natick, ya gonna feel tiyahed, and maybe ya pahtnah will feel tiyahed, but remembah that you trained fuh this and you got this. At this point you can grab a Cliff bah and some watah to give you a boost of energy. Throw the watah in ya face if ya have to. Bring ya fingah up to ya pahtnah's shouldah blade, as if ya passin' through Wellesley, ovah to the othah shouldah like ya in Newton. You always gotta remembah to keep a steady pace. It's a marathon, nawt a sprint. Bring ya fingah up the back of theah neck like ya in Brookline, and then push through to thetawp of theah head like you just crossed the finish line in Kenmore Square. Disclaimah: absolutely do nawt, undah any circumstances, try to wrap a penis in a foil blanket aftah this. Also, it should go without sayin', but Gatorade does nawt make fuh good lube.

Although it feels like you may have done a lawt of work, remembah that was still only just a wahwm-up to the real deal. Nawt only is it a very practical tool to help excite ya pahtnah, but it's also a fun and infohmative lesson on the Bawston Marathon runnah's route.

Ahnuhthah way to excite ya pahtnah is to kiss and suck on theah neck until you give them a hickey. That's right, you read that right, a *hickey*. Most grown adults ah wicked embarrassed by hickeys, but in Bawston we feel exactly opposite! Hickeys are a badge of honah! You gotta weah 'em proud, just like a rainbow flag on pride day. Except, instead of a rainbow flag on pride day, it's more of like a brownish circle on ya neck ya weah on Saturdays aftah a good Friday night. But, you can weah one on any weekday really if ya crazy like that.

Sometimes, while ya havin' sex you might make some choices that you regret aftah, but a hickey should nevah be one. Everyone knows that gettin' ya neck sucked on a little feels wicked good, and nothin' says, "Hey. Look at me. I just got my neck sucked," like a hickey. So throw away those stupid-lookin' turtlenecks frum the '90s, take awff that scaaf in July, and show that beautiful brown suction cup–lookin' sex symbol. Hickey's ah nawt just a product of what happens when horny high schoolahs go see a movie. Hickey's ah fur everyone and anyone who wants to stand up at a PTA meeting and say, "Yeah. I'm a mothah of five and, yeah, I still know how to get freaky."

Light biting can be a good way to open up ya pahtnah's senses and exploah a new way of bein' a bit moah dangerous without actually hurtin' each othah. Light biting is like dipin' ya toe in the S/M pool. You wanna be freaky, but you also don't like gettin' on all foahs while ya pahtnah hits you with a paddle and calls you a good little poodle. The key to biting is to gauge how much ya patnah wants, and also to keep the pressha easy and don't go too hahd. Theah is a sayin' in Bawston when it comes to bitin', "Keep it light. Keep it light, when ya bite." A good way to remembah that sayin' is to rhyme it with the lyrics, "Get it ripe, get it right, get it tight," and the tune frum the evah-so-populah Bubba Sparxxx song, "Ms. New Booty."

If that's too much to remembah, or if you just plain don't like that Bubba Sparxxx hit song frum 2006, just be shoah to keep an open dialogue with ya pahtnah. Some pahts of the bawdy that ah good to give some love and light biting ah:

- The thighs.
- The tummy.
- The nipples.
- The neck.
- The back of the neck.

- The chest.

- The shouldahs.

- The biceps.

Some pahts of the bawdy that ah nevah good to bite, nawt even lightly, ah:

- The Frank.

- The Munchkins of a Frank.

- The Donut.

- The Sprinkle of a Donut.

- The webbing between ya toes.

- The toenails.

- The fingahnails.

- The calf muscles.

- The ahmpits.

- The backs of the knees.

- The ankles.

- The eyelids, eyeballs, or anywheah neah the eyes. Like, what the fuck? Ah you crazy?

- The wenis.

Again, what is most impohtant is that you always keep an open line of communication with the person ya havin' sex with befoah and durin' sex. Whethah you've been datin' fur a long time, or ya havin' a one-night stand, ya gotta always respect the wishes of ya pahtnah. Sex is a two-way street and ya can't be selfish, especially when it comes to bein' adventurous with foah play. Befoah havin' sex, talk about what ya into and what ya nawt into. Talk about what ya willin' to try and what you are absolutely nevah gonna do. Who knows, maybe you'll find out that ya actually do like gettin' on all foahs and gettin' slapped with a paddle while ya pahtnah calls ya a good little poodle. And maybe, just maybe, you'll even let someone lightly bite ya wenis.

CHAPTAH 9:

WHAT AH OTHAH THINGS I CAN DO WITH MY FENWAY FRANK OR DUNKIN' DONUT?

Aftah foahplay comes what Bawstonians like to call, "Fun Play." Fun Play includes any and all othah fun things that one can do with theah pahtnah and theah pahtnah's junk beyond sex. Sexual penetration between The Frank and The Donut is always gonna be magical, but it doesn't have to be so limiting. Don't think of sex as only two bland colors of black and white. Theah ah so many different shades of gray to exploah in between. Accoahdin' to E. L. James theah is even, like, fifty of 'em. Why does she use the numbah fifty, anyway? That's so many shades. Like, why nawt twenty-three or, like, forty-one? Sorry, I digress. What really mattahs is that theah is moah than one way to enjoy The Frank and The Donut beyond basic penetration.

We Bawstonians refah to a penis as a Fenway Frank and a vagina as a Dunkin' Donut because, much like an actual Fenway Frank and Dunkin' Donut, theah are a lawt of metaphoahs we can use to talk about them both in public without soundin' too dirty. Just make shoah ya nevah actually try and put ketchup on ya penis, or icing on ya vagina. Unless ya into that kind of thing, then do whatevah floats ya crazy little boat.

With The Frank, you can give it pleasha by kissin', and lickin', and slidin' it in and out of ya mouth. You can lightly hold The Frank with one or, depending if it's a foot-long, maybe two hands. You can move yah hand up and down, lightly applying pressha, to get it real nice and hahd. Just like with a hawt dawg, you can also apply condiments to make ya man's Frank taste bettah. Let's be frank about Franks, they ain't all gonna taste amazing. Some are old, some have probably been dropped on the floah of the kitchen, and some have probably been handled by some dirty-ass hands. If this is the case, applyin' some safe and approved flavored lube is always a good choice. Besides, no one eats a real Fenway Frank just as it is right out of the package. Ya gotta get that ketchup, mustahd, and relish on theah to make it extra tasty. Although, if ya real hungry fuh that Frank and ya haven't had one in a while ya might get excited and just eat it "raw dawg."

"Raw Dawg" is what we call it when ya put The Frank in and around somebody's orifices without any bun. A bun, obviously bein' code word fur a condom. Stay with me heah. Now, you can eat The Frank raw dawg, but you must proceed with extreme caution, because theah ah STIs out theah that you can get even frum just eatin' The Frank or The Donut. And ya gotta be extra careful when goin' raw dawg *into* The Donut. Ya can nevah be shoah about those little hawt dawg juices and you don't want that Donut becomin' a filled-up Bawston cream donut. Bawston creams ah fuckin delicious, and a gift frum Gawd, but only when you want one. Nawt everyone likes Bawston creams, especially parents who have teenagahs.

With The Donut, ya gotta give it some love and handle it with care. As anyone frum Bawston can tell ya, Donuts ah worshipped across the city. They ah sometimes put on a very high pedestal, which makes it that much moah stressful fuh someone who wants to enjoy one. Howevah, ya can't be intimidated by The Donut. Ya gotta embrace The Donut and all its complexities.

Befoah gettin' to sex, be shoah to give it some love by holdin' it gently and lickin around its curves. You can stick ya tongue in and out and lick the innah walls to lick up that sweet icing. If some of the icing is about to drip awff, ya can use ya fingahs to gently brush it up into ya mouth. This visual can be very exciting fuh some women. Whenevah ya get an original unglazed donut, ya gonna need to give it some love and care. It's gonna be a little dry, and this requiahs some extra patience and attention with ya tongue. Get to know it, make it feel beautiful, and befoah ya know it, that original unglazed donut will be like a glazed donut fresh out the oven. Or microwave? Nawt really shoah how the actual Dunkin' Donuts bakes theah donuts—whatevah! You get the analogy. MOVING ON!

When ya pleashurin' The Donut, just be shoah that it's nawt a jelly-filled one. Sometimes, when ya real excited, you'll go fur any donut ya see and nawt realize ya picked a jelly-filled one. Although an actual jelly-filled Donut is extremely delicious, in Bawston a jelly-filled Donut usually refahs to a woman on her period. We know that probably just ruined jelly-filled Donuts fuh you furevah, but that's just what we call it. Get used to it.

So, next time ya in Bawston and a girl says, "Sorry, I can't have sex right now 'cause my Donut is filled with jelly," you'll know that she's nawt talkin' about the delicious treat she just bawt. Although theah is a chance that she might have an actual jelly donut that just got everywheah all ovah her bedsheets and that's why she can't have sex. But, more awften than nawt, she's talkin' about her period. Remembah, this only applies to women frum Bawston. If ya live anywheah else in the world and you ask a woman if her Donut is filled with jelly, she's probably just gonna get confused and think ya callin' her fat. Which would most absolutely lead to no sex fuh you.

The key to gettin' The Frank and The Donut excited is to always handle them with care. These ah beloved foods in Bawston, and like any beloved food, ya don't just gobble 'em down. Ya get them when ya feelin' a little naughty and ya wanna take ya time with them. What's also impohtant is that ya practice nevah havin' too much of a good thing. Again, it's good to enjoy a treat, but only once in a while and nawt all the time. Ya gonna wanna give it a rest in between snackin'. Take ya time to choose the right treat and you'll enjoy it just as much the next time around when ya have it. Once you've done all this, you ah now ready fuh sex.

CHAPTAH 10:

WHAT AH SOME SEXUAL POSITIONS TO SPICE UP MY SEX LIFE?

By now, you ah ready fuh the main attraction. The Guinness to ya St. Paddy's Day Parade. The clam to ya chowdah. The home run to ya Fenway Park. You get the idea. Ovah the yeahs, Bawstonians have made a name fuh themselves in the bedroom. We are adventurous, we are unafraid to exploah, and we ah loud, very, very loud. How-evah, we have nawt always been this way.

Theah was a time when the indigenous Americans who lived in Bawston used to use many different sexual positions and were very open and free about theah bodies. But when John Eliot and the rest of the Puritans came ovah frum England, they were missionaries who only practiced missionary.

Luckily, ovah the yeahs, and mostly because of Ben Franklin, Bawstonians evolved as sexual bein's to incorporate some diversity in the bedroom. We'ah no longah the witch-burnin', Gawd-fearin' Christians you have come to know and love. Shoah, we ah still a little racist in pahts, but we'ah tryin' ah best to fix that. The good news is that we have become much moah diverse in the bedroom. Ah sexual lexicon is growin' and wicked complex, just like the word "lexicon." Anyways, heah ah some sexual positions, straight frum Bawston, to help guide you on ya journey to obtaining wicked good sex.

Heah ah some sexual positions wheah the man is moah dominant when havin' sex with a woman:

The Bawston Common - The woman lies flat on her back as if she is sunbathin' on the grass. The man mounts her frum the tawp, like classic missionary, and once his Frank is inside her Donut, the two will barrel roll to the left and then to the right. Doin' so will simulate them rollin' down a hill in the Commons. Fur added pleasha, feel free to throw in some trash or used heroin needles on ya bed to simulate the actual fields of the Commons. If ya feelin' frisky, ya can even invite a homeless guy frum awff the street to come in and watch you have sex while he mastahbates in the cornah. Or, to save you time and energy, you can just have sex in the actual Boston Commons, but just be cahful nawt to get arrested.

The Make Way fuh Ducklings - The woman lies flat on her back, and opens her legs wide like the flyin' V shape ducks make when they fly south fuh the wintah. The man, frum the bottom of the bed, squats down on his feet and waddles towahds her like a duckling. The man should really get into the role-play heah and feel free to quack like a little duckling. Now, it should be noted that theah is a fine line between this bein' really sexy and also really friggin' creepy. If the man does it right, the woman will love it and think it's wicked cute. If the man does it wrong, then he will look like an insane person. As the man approaches the woman, he remains squatting on his feet, and begins to move his Frank in and out of the woman's Donut. This action should mimic like when little ducks poke theah heads into pond watah tryin' to snatch up little fishies.

The Paul Revere Midnight Ride - This position is nawt influenced by the size of the man's Frank. He can be a Hancock, a State, or a Revere. What is impohtant is that the man embrace his love fuh history and remembah that impohtant night when Paul Revere warned the sleeping town of Bawston of the incoming British attack. The woman lies in the fetal position, with her eyes closed, as if she is fast asleep. The man will then jump on the bed, wake her up, and flip her up and around so her hands and knees are on the bed. The man will approach her frum behind, insert his Frank in her Donut, and ride her like a hoahse while screamin' out, "The British ah comin'! The British ah comin'!" To add a little more excitement to this move, you can have a foahsome with a British couple, and have them mimic the position directly behind you as if they'ah chasin' you on hoahseback. When they staht actually cumming, they can then join you as well in screaming out, "We'ah comin'! Gawd damn' it, it feels so good, we'ah comin'!"

The Bawston Massacre – Disclaimah: this position is fur all the men out theah who ah sadomasochists. It might nawt work too well if ya nawt into gettin' spit on or havin' things thrown at ya in the bedroom. Fuh this position, the woman stands up, with her back against a wall, and the man stands in front of her and begins to mastahbate with his Frank. He does so until he is about to orgasm, and right as he is about to, the woman stahts to yell at him. She can spit on him, throw things at him, and say things like, "C'mon ya British bastahd, fiyah ya weapon. Do it!" If the man is nawt into the yelling and spitting, the woman can also just stand theah, and wait fuh him to fire awff his Frank. Once fired upon, she can really ham up her acting skills and fall to the ground as if wounded.

The Bawston Tea Party - The woman lies down on her back on the bed. The man surprises the woman by jumping into the bed dressed up as a Native American. He then squats down, hovahs his Frank ovah the womans face, and lightly dips his ball sack down onto her face. The woman can then kiss and suck on the mans Frank and ball sack as he stands up, squats down, stands up, and continues this repetitive action.

The Red Sox - The woman lies flat on her back, bends her knees towahds her stomach, and lifts her feet up in the aiyah. The man smacks the woman's feet with his Frank until her feet get kinda red, like red sox. The man then inserts his Frank into the woman's Donut, as she keeps her feet in the aiyah and smacks his back with them to keep them red. Just as the guy is about to orgasm, the woman pushes him awff her, and says, "Sorry, maybe next yeah." When the man is defeated and in so much pain frum blue balls, the woman then says, "Just kiddin' get in here!" and allows him to orgasm inside her Donut. This sexual position can be frustrating fuh the man, make him real angry, and mess with his head, but that's why we call it the Red Sox.

The Bill Buckner - The woman stands on the bed in a crouched position, like a first baseman. The man lies undahneath the woman, lifts his pelvis up, and supports his weight with his ahms. He then begins to swing his Frank back and foahth, grazing the woman's Donut, but nevah inserting his Frank into it. The trick is fuh the man to tease the woman as if he is goin' to insert it, but he nevah does. To add to the excitement, the woman can also place her hands out in front of her as if she is goin' to try and catch The Frank. But alas, she nevah does.

The Yawkey Way - Fuh this experience to be effective, it's best if the man and woman stand upright in a crowded coat closet. Be shoah to let light in so ya nawt in dahkness. The man will stand behind the woman and insert his Frank into her Donut frum behind. As they have sex, they'll be bumpin' into coats, and this will act as a realistic experience as to how Gawd damn crowded Yawkey Way can get befoah and aftah a game. The man and woman, while enjoyin' sex, can both yell at the coats, "Fuck awff!" and "Get the fuck outta my way, ya prick!" This position is great fur any Bawstonian lookin' to have angry sex.

The Babe - The woman lies flat on her back with her bawdy straight down on the bed. The man lies on tawp of her, in classic missionary position, and inserts his Frank into her Donut. Just as he is about to orgasm, the man stands up directly ovah the woman, and points to a spawt on her bawdy. He then finishes his orgasm by stroking his Frank, and as he ejaculates he tries to hit the paht of the woman's bawdy that he pointed to befoah. If the man is successful in hittin' the exact spawt he pointed to, then everyone who heahs of it will call him a "Great Bambino." Women take note, a man who loves this position and is good at hittin' his mahk isn't trustworthy. Men who ah good at this position awften get cawky, have no loyalty, and will up and leave ya at the drop of a hat.

The Dane Cook "SuFi"- If you evah seen one of Dane Cook's stand-up comedy specials, and let's face it ya probably did, you know the "SuFi" as the name Dane Cook gave fur a "supah middle fingah." In this position, the woman lies down flat on her back with her bawdy straight down on the bed. The man, somewhat cawky and with a big sense of confidence fuh someone just stahtin' out in the bedroom, approaches the woman and inserts his middle and ring fingah into her Donut. The man can then use both fingahs to go in and out of the woman's Donut and rub around in circulah motions. The man must make shoah that these ah nawt vicious circulah motions, but nice and easy. The SuFi was wicked populah in Bawston, and all ovah the United States in 2006, but then, like two yeahs latah, it was hated by everyone. Bawstonians still kinda like this position, even though everyone makes them feel bad fuh liking it. Howevah, those people who make Bawstonians feel bad fuh liking it probably loved it at one time too, and maybe still think it's a little fun, but will nevah admit that they still like it, nor nevah have they evah liked it, fuh feah of bein' outcasted frum society.

The Steve Carell - A hometown favorite, because it's gentle and sweet just like the comedian it's named aftah. The woman sits in an awffice chaiyah, and the man straddles her legs. The man inserts his Frank, frum an upwahd angle, into the woman's Donut. It may be a tight fit. This position is best if the woman is a Big Dig and the guy is a Revere. To make this position more authentic, the woman might want to try this with a forty-year-old virgin man. Although this position is also a fan favorite across the world, and mostly done in L.A., it nevah fuhgets its roots back in Bawston. It's also a big hit in Marshfield durin' the summah.

The Tom Brady - Women go crazy fuh this one. Men ah jealous of othah men who get to do this position, because it's wicked hahd to do and takes a lawt of athleticism and endurance. This position is best done on a solid flooah wheah theah is a lawt of space next to ya bed. The woman bends ovah and touches her toes, and the man stands behind her. He yells, "Ready, set, hike!" and quickly inserts his Frank into the woman's Donut, picks her up frum the waist, and then lifts her in the aiyah. The man then runs in place while his Frank goes in and out of the woman's Donut until they both orgasm. Aftah both man and woman orgasm, the man will sometimes spike the woman down on the bed and yell, "Touchdown!" A lawt of othah cities hate this position, but it's mostly because they'ah just jealous of how good it is in the bedroom. It's always a winnin' move and Bawstonian guys will nevah try it unless theah balls ah fully inflated.

The Bill Belichick - Some may say that this position is only fuh cheatahs, and those people ah just fuckin' dicks. They have nevah had good sex befoah, and they just don't know what it's like to be on top. Fuh this postion, the woman lies flat with her bawdy straight on the bed and her legs at a nintey degree angle in the aiyah. The man lies with his stomach on the woman's feet, suspended in the aiyah, so that his naked bawdy is like the football on tawp of the The Vince Lombardi trophy. Then the woman will yell out, "Fuck you, Jets!" and open her legs to a *V* position. At that moment, the man will fall through her legs, come flyin' down, and insert his Frank rapidly into her Donut. This is a classic move that has been around Bawston fuh moah than seventeen yeahs. Some even say that the Patriots use a variation of the move to increase leg strength when trainin' in the end of summah befoah the new season stahts. You'll feel just like a Patriot doin' this move, except you'll be naked and nawt worth a ton of money.

The Flyin' Bobby Orr - One moment comes to everyone's mind when they heah the name Bobby Orr. This sexual position is based awff the iconic photo taken in 1970 when Bobby Orr, aftah shootin' the winning goal to bring home the Stanley Cup fuh the Bruins, was tripped and captchahd mid-flight. To replicate that image, the woman lies flat on her stomach with her bawdy straight out on the bed. The man lies directly on tawp of the woman with his stomach on her back, facin' the same way. The man inserts his Frank frum behind into the woman's Donut and togethah they will rock foahwahd and backwahd. Just as the man is about to climax, the woman will push herself up on her hands and knees. The man will remain flat and extend both ahms and legs as if he is mid-flight, just like one of the greats. If ya feel comf'table enough, you can even invite a friend ovah to take a pic of this tricky maneuvah. It is truly breathtaking.

The Battle Of Bunker Hill – The man stands on tawp of the bed, and the woman stands on the ground beside the bed. Fuh historical accuracy, the man can also be wearin' an outft that resembles a minuteman, and the woman can weah a red coat to resemble the British. The woman massages the man's Frank until it is wicked hahd. The man will try to hold back his climax as long as he can. By doin' so, he'll be saving his ammunition for when he needs it most. A man doesn't awften know when he'll find himself in battle, so it's good fur him to know that he's saved up, to make it feel so much bettah when he finally gets to fiyah awff some rounds. Once he's close to climaxing, he will take hold of his Frank and orgasm onto the woman's face. In the famous Battle of Bunker Hill, it was said that the colonial forces were told, "Don't fire until you see the whites of their eyes." But in this case, when the man fiyahs, the woman should close her eyes so as nawt to be forced to have an extremely awkwahd convahsation with her optometrist the next day.

Heah ah some sexual positions wheah the woman is moah dominant when havin' sex with a man:

The *Cheers* - Just like the famous show, everyone should know each othah's names if they'ah takin' paht in this sexual position. The man lies flat on his back and the woman sits at the bottom of the bed neah his feet. She massages his Frank until it's wicked hahd, and then, just as he is about to climax, she pulls it straight down like a beeah tap and inserts it into her Donut. People frum Bawston know and love this position, but only because of the show and nawt because of the actual bah. To be completely awnest, I don't think one true native of Bawston has evah stepped inside Cheers befoah. If they did, it was probably just to use the bathroom frum a day at the Public Gardens.

The Two-Way Street - This position is nawt very cawmmon in Bawston, mostly because the city is filled with one-way streets. Only a woman decides if she wants to do this, and it is nevah up to the man. The man will lie down flat on his back with his bawdy straight down on the bed. The woman will face away frum the man, mount him, straddling his legs, and insert his Frank into her Donut. While she rides him, she will take a long Dunkin' Donuts Pretzel Twist and insert it into her chocolate Donut. A chocolate Donut is code fuh butt hole. A Dunkin' Donut Pretzel Twist is literally a Dunkin' Donut Pretzel Twist.

Bawston women love 'em. If the man climaxes too soon, the woman can continue using the Dunkin' Donut Pretzel Twist in both her Donut and chocolate Donut. She should be shoah to make use of her two-way streets to reach the full potential pleasha and help her to orgasm.

The South Station - The key to this position is fuh the woman to be quick and agile. The real South Station is a very busy hub with trains and buses coming and goin' at all houahs of the day, and it's especially busy durin' rush houah. The man lies flat on his back with his bawdy straight out on the bed. The woman will shout, "All aboahd!" and then jump on tawp of the man, straddle his legs, and insert his Frank in her Donut. She'll ride him fur a bit, then jump awff. She'll move her face down to his Frank, shout, "All aboahd!" and then suck on The Frank. Then she'll flip around to face away frum the man, sit on tawp of him, straddle his legs with her legs, and yell once moah, "All aboahd!" Then she'll insert his Frank into her Donut and ride him as she faces away frum him. This rapid sequence of position changes replicates how trains quickly entah and leave the tracks at South Station. Just as the woman is about to climax, she will jump awff the man, grab his head, push it down south, and have him lick her Sprinkle. Sprinkle is code fuh clitoris. When the woman is about to orgasm, she will sometimes yell out, "Final stawp, orgasm town! Pawpulation me!"

The Amy Poehler - The woman is a total bawss heah. She owns the room, just like the comedienne this position is named aftah. The woman sits in a chaiyah at a desk, the man gets on his hands and knees undah the desk, and the woman straddles the man's head with her legs. The woman grabs the man's head and brings it in close to her Donut, and makes him kiss, massage, and lick her Sprinkle while she says some of the best one-linahs, like, "Have I seen you around heah befoah? The tawp of ya head looks familiyah," and, "That feels amazing! I didn't know you could read lips." To add a little moah fun into the mix, the woman can invite her friend frum Philly to come and join her fur a real one two punch. If this position is done late on a Saturday night, we call it **The Weekend Cumdate.**

The Mike's Famous Cannoli - The man stands outside the bedroom doah and massages his Frank to get himself excited. Inside the bedroom, on the othah side of the doah, the woman is massaging her Donut and Sprinkle. The woman then peeks her head out to the man and says, "It's gonna be like a fifteen-minute wait." The man, a little bummed out, remains excited and eagah to do the Mike's Famous Cannoli position. He continues to massage his Frank. When the woman is close to climaxing, she opens the doah and the man runs in, jumps on the bed, and lies flat on his back. The woman massages his Frank rapidly, and just as they ah both about to orgasm, the woman ties a blue string with a bow around the base of the man's Frank. This prolongs his orgasm, and increases the size of The Frank, which the woman then quickly inserts into her Donut. Aftah inserting The Frank into her Donut, the woman can pull the string, releasing the bow and allowing them to orgasm at the same time with a wicked sick intensity. It is a feelin' that reminds the man and woman why it was very much worth the wait.

The Whitey - The man sits on a cawnah of the bed, and the woman straddles his legs. The woman faces away frum the man and puts her hands behind her back as if she is bein' arrested fuh tons of crimes and runnin' frum the law fuh many yeahs. The woman then inserts the man's Frank into her Donut. She moves her bawdy up and down as if she's tryin' to get away frum him, and she can even play up the role a bit and yell obscenities back at him, like, "You suck! You dirty FBI rat! Do you know who I am?!? I'll have you killed fuh this!" The woman can then stand up as if she is tryin' one last time to break free, but the man will pull her close to him, pushin' his Frank against her Sprinkle, and this helps her to orgasm.

The Dropkick Murphy - The man stands upright beside the bed, and the woman kneels befoah him. She blows on his Munchkins and massages his Frank as if it's a bagpipe. The man can stomp on the ground to keep a steady beat and pump up the energy. The woman can also join in and bang her fists against the man's thighs to keep the steady beat. This pounding will help to bring the hahd-core metal vibes to the bedroom to simulate The Dropkick Murphys actually bein' theah in person. The woman will then stand up, and now that both man and woman ah standing, the woman will insert the man's Frank into her Donut, and they will both jump up and down togethah and head bang. This position is best done with "I'm Shipping Up to

Boston" blarin' on full blast.

The Duck Tour - The man lies faceup on the bed with his elbows and feet supportin' his weight so his bawdy is lifted just a few inches awff the bed. The woman mounts the man, facing him, straddling his hips with her legs, and inserts his Frank into her Donut. As the woman rides back and foahth, she can pull out a megaphone and give him a history lesson about the city of Bawston and talk about all its famous landmahks. As the woman does this, the man pulsates his bawdy as if he is a giant cah drivin' on tawp the cawbblestone streets of Bawston. Just as the woman is about to climax, the man will then lift his bawdy up into the aiyah, liftin' the woman wicked high. Disclaimah: this position can hit the woman's Donut in a unique way which will lead her to squirt. This is called the "Splashdown," named aftah what the actual Duck Tours call it when the ride splashes down into the Charles River. If ya evah visit Bawston, fuhget about buyin' tickets to the Duck Tours because this position is the real thing.

The Christmas Tree Shawp – Women LOVE the Christmas Tree Shawp position. Men like it too, secretly, but it is a fact that the women of Bawston love this position because it's designed to get a two-fur-one deal. You can do this position 365 days a yeah, but it's the most fun around the Christmas holiday season. With this position, the woman will wrap up her bottom half with Christmas wrapping papah like a miniskirt, as if it is a present. Side note, it is a present because it's ya Donut and every Bawstonian man loves a nicely wrapped up Donut. The woman then gets on all foahs on the bed. The man approaches her frum behind and unwraps her, and then goes back and foath between toungin' her chocolate Donut and her Donut. The man then inserts his Frank frum behind, stahtin' with her Donut and then moving to her chocolate Donut. This two fur one deal is a fan favorite of most women because, just like with the actual Christmas Tree Shawp, everyone loves a bahgain.

The Phantom Gourmet – Based on one of the best shows in American/Bawston television. Theah is nothin' bettah than goin' out on a date with someone ya love to a restaurant knowin' The Phantom was theah and gave it a good review. In this position, the woman lies down on her dinin' room table. The man approaches in a cape and mask as if he's The Phantom. He'll staht to kiss and softly bite the woman up and down her entiyah bawdy like she's a scrumptious meal that he's tryin' fuh the first time. The woman will then serve The Phantom the main coahse, which is her Donut. She'll force his head into her lap so she can enshoah that she'll get a good rating and that The Phantom thoroughly enjoys her gourmet fare. If you are a woman and want to make this position even more exciting, do this with someone you just met. This will be shoah to add a bit more excitement and intrigue to the evening.

Jordan's Furniture – Everybawdy frum Bawston, grownups and kids alike, love to go to Jordan's Furniture. Nawt just fuh the discounted furnitcha, but also because some of them had the 4-D motion rides. Those rides ah pretty awesome, but if you are a woman frum Bawston, this position is even bettah. It's a throwback to a classic you loved frum ya childhood, but you also get to orgasm, which is wicked sick. In this position, the man sits in an awffice chaiyah, preferably one that has an attachment that doubles the awffice chaiyah as a massage chaiyah. The woman sits on the man's lap, facing away frum him, and inserts his Frank into her Donut. The man grabs the woman's hands in his hands so that her ahms ah resting on his like he's the motion chaiyah frum a Jordan's Furniture 4-D motion ride. The man then bumps up and down, moves frum side to side, and dips foahwahd and backwahd. The man will begin to pick up speed and move more intensely to increase pleasha to the woman frum all angles. To heighten the experience, the man and woman can weah virtual reality headsets and watch a poahn video. The man can even mimic the motion in the poahn. This experience will spoil ya, 'cause you'll nevah be able to ride the 4-D rollah coastah at Jordan's Furniture again.

The House of the Seven Gables – This position requiyahs moah than one man, and the woman has to be comf'table with dominating moah than one man at a time. To most Bawston women, this should come pretty easily. Seven men will lie down on theah backs, in whichevah foahmation is easiest and comf'table, in an area of a house wheah theah is lots of room. Each man will hold up theah erect Frank in one hand and a dildo in the othah hand. The men will make the dildo tips touch the tips of theah Franks as if to imitate the look of a gable on a house. The woman will then go around to each man and insert both the dildo and his Frank into her Donut. She'll visit each "gable" to get the most pleasha. This position is best fuh women who ah considahd to be a Big Dig. Theah is a variation of this move fuh women who ah Pavilions or Fenways, and it's called **The House of the Seven Chimneys.** It's nawt as exciting, but it's a little bit easiyah to accomplish because with this variation, the men all hold the dildos upright next to theah Franks to mimic the shape of chimneys. It's a little less populah.

Heah ah some sexual positions fuh two men, and the roles can be swapped depending on who prefers to be moah dominant:

The Fenway Frank Bun Wrap - One of the men will stand upright and approach the bed. As he approaches the bed, holding his Frank in his hand, he yells out, "Hawt dawgs fuh sale! Get ya hawt dawgs heah!" The othah man sits on the cawnah of the bed with his back upright, waiving a condom in one hand, and yells back, "Ovah heah! I'll take one!" The man sitting on the bed then wraps the othah man's Frank with the condom as if it's a hawt dawg bun. He massages and sucks the man's Frank until the man orgasms into the bun. Remindah: the bun is the condom and nawt an actual bun.

The Castle Island - The real Castle Island has been the site of a fortification since 1634, but the sexual position has been the focus of fornification since 1951. Based awff the evah populah Sullivan's, or

"Sullie's" if ya frum Southie, located at Castle Island, this position is a fan favorite. Both men lie on theah sides with theah heads at opposite ends of the bed so theah mouths are aligned with each othah's Franks. Both men will suck each othah's Frank supah fast as if they ah Sullie's hawt dawgs and they have been waitin' all wintah just to get one. A remindah to any men that ah interested in tryin' this position: do nawt eat the Frank too quickly or else you will choke. Sullie's has made it very cleah that they are only responsible fuh theah actual food and will nawt be held liable fuh any injuries caused by this sex position.

The Sons of Liberty - Both men stand upright and place an effigy doll of a politician who is a piece of shit on the cawnah of the bed. In unison and solidarity, they staht to massage each othah's Frank and continue to do so until they both orgasm all ovah the effigy doll. Immediately aftah, both men will throw feathahs at the doll, light it on fiyah, and then throw it out the bedroom window. Always be shoah to practice extreme cawtion when lightin' an effigy doll on fiyah, 'cause feathahs and semen are extremely flammable.

The L Street Bathhouse – Cleanliness of bawdy is next to Gawdliness, and that's the motto fuh this position. Both men stand upright togethah in the showah, like the L Street Brownies did way back in the mid-nineteenth century. One man inserts his Frank into the othah's chocolate Donut frum behind, and togethah they move up and down as they clean theah bodies in the showah. What's good about this position is that you can kill two birds with one stone. Ya gettin' down and dirty, but also keepin' ya bawdy clean. Fuh an extra twist on this move, use ice-cold watah on New Yeah's Day to pay homage to the L Street Brownies who would plunge into the icy-cold watah in Dorchester Bay on New Yeah's Day. It's definitely nawt fuh the weak skinned, and ya gotta be a bit of a masochist.

St. Paddy's Day Bagpiper - One man stands upright and holds the othah man by the waist upside down so that the theah resepective Franks are aligned with each othah's mouths. The man standin' holds the upside-down man with one ahm around the waist, and the othah ahm around the leg. The man standin' upright inserts the othah man's Frank into his mouth and begins to blow him like a true fiyahfightah playin' a bagpipe on one of the drunkest holidays in Bawston. As he continues to blow the upside-down man's Frank, he can also squeeze the man's buttocks to really get a nice tune out of him. Legend has it, ten men frum Southie perfoahmed this position in unison in 1984, and it was the most beautiful thing anyone has evah seen in Bawston.

The Steven Tyler - One man wraps a satin scaaf around his Frank and fashions it to look like Steven Tyler's microphone. The man then does a handstand and acts as if his bawdy is the mic stand and his Frank is the microphone. Pro tip: the man acting as the microphone is gonna wanna have a strawng uppah bawdy and really good balance to pull it awff. The othah man walks up, confidently, and grabs him by his Frank. The man standin' upright sucks on the upside-down man's Frank and rocks it back and foahth. As he does this, the man perfoahmin' the handstand sings the entiyahty of Aerosmith's "Dream On." As he is about to climax, the man perfoahmin' the handstand gets loudah and loudah and continues to build with the natural progression of the song. As the man in the handstand stahts to orgasm, both men in unison belt out the final, "DREAM ON! DREAM ON! DREAM UNTIL YA DREAMS CUM TRUE!"

The Good Will Hunting - Just like the very real bromance between Ben Affleck and Matt Damon in the movie, this position will bring two men closah togethah than evah befoah. One man stands bent ovah with his ahms on the bed. The othah man stands behind him and inserts his Frank into his pahtnah's chocolate Donut. The man on tawp draws with a Sharpie on the othah man's back as if he is tryin' to solve an equation. He can actually be tryin' to solve an equation, or just drawin' numbahs, it really doesn't mattah. The man who is bent ovah reaches back to his Frank and massages it, grabbing his Munchkins. As he does this, he yells back at the man takin' him frum behind, "How do you like them apples?"

The Bawston Cream Pie – Prep time fuh this position is about fifteen minutes. You'll need to get some ingredients and tools including: a condom, a whisk, one ounce of unsweetened chocolate, and a human-sized cooling rack. One man props up on all foahs on the bed with his chocolate Donut up in the aiyah. The othah man positions himself on his knees behind the othah man. The man on his knees will wrap his Frank in a condom and insert it into the othah man's chocolate Donut, thrusting it in and out. As he does this, he will lay the unsweetened chocolate on the othah man's back. Heat will be produced on the man's back frum all the sex, and the chocolate will melt in a delicious-looking pattern. The man on his knees can then use the whisk to lightly spank the othah man and stir the melted chocolate on his back. The man on his knees orgasms inside the othah man and then pulls out his Frank, but leaves the condom in. The man who was on all foahs can then lay himself down on the cooling rack to enjoy the sensation of cooling awff as a human Bawston Cream Pie.

The Charles River - One man lies on his back with his bawdy straight down on the bed. The othah man stands directly ovah him, and both men massage theah Franks. As both are about to climax, the man who is standin' positions his Frank right at the tawp of the othah man's chest. The standin' man orgasms down the othah man's chest, and the semen travels down his pahtnah's bawdy just like the Charles River. The man who is lyin' down orgasms onto his stomach, and his semen hits the othah man's semen as if it's the meeting between the Charles River and the rough watahs of the Bawston Harbor. When done right, the two forces of semen crash togethah and make waves. It's absolute poetry in motion.

The Geronimo – If you've evah been to Water Country up in New Hampshire, you know that Geronimo is one of the best rides they have in the pahk. Fuh this position, both men stand on tawp of the bed. One man approaches the othah frum behind and inserts his

Frank. They have sex standin' on the bed. Just as the man frum behind is about to climax, he grabs the waist of the man in front of him, and the man in front curls up into a ball, like a canon ball. As the man frum behind climaxes, he yells out, "Geronimo!" He jumps into the aiyah and slams down both bawdies onto the bed. Although Water Country is up in New Hampshire, Bawstonians know it and love it as one of theah own. Howevah, if you are a proud Bawstonian and hate to admit you love Water Country ovah Water Wizz, then the next position is a variation fuh you.

The Pirate's Plunge – Just like The Geronimo, but fuh the Bawstonians that want to stay true to Water Wizz and the Cape, the Pirate's Plunge is a fan favorite of men frum Bawston. Both men sit up in a bathtub, with one man sitting on the othah man's lap. The man on bottom inserts his Frank into the othah man's chocolate Donut and begins to move up and down. Just as the man frum behind is about to climax, he grabs the othah man's waist, and the man on tawp curls up into a ball, like a cannon ball. The man on the bottom then holds his breath, plunges beneath the watah, and climaxes while undah watah.

The Midnight Ride – Although the original midnight ride was made by the patriots Paul Revere, William Dawes, and Dr. Samuel Prescott, this Midnight Ride is somewhat different. It's hahd to say if the original Midnight Ride involved sex between the three patriots, but it most likely did nawt. In this variation on The Paul Revere Midnight

Ride, one man gets on all foahs on the bed like a hoahse. Fuh the full effect, this man can even chew on an apple or a sugah cube. You do whatevah works fuh you. The othah man then runs into the room and jumps onto the bed, quickly inserting his Frank into his pahtnah's chocolate Donut. As this happens, the man on all foahs will buck and neigh like a hoahse. The man behind him will ride him like his life and the lives of his countrymen depend on it. This position is best fur an orgy, with foah othah men pretending to be the othah Midnight Ridahs and hoahses.

Heah ah some sexual positions fuh two women, and the roles can be swapped depending on who prefers to be moah dominant:

Beantown – Usually, a woman's clitoris would be refahd to as her Sprinkle, but in some instances Bawston women prefeah to call it a Bean. This is one of the moah basic, but classic, positions fuh women in Bawston. It became such a classic that they decided to name it aftah the populah nickname given to Bawston. One woman lies flat on her back on the bed. The othah woman lies facedown on tawp of her pahtnah so that both of theah mouths are against the othah's Donut. They count down togethah, "Three, two, one!" and then they both race to see who can get the othah person to orgasm first. This race to the finish is awften refahed to in Bawston as "goin' to Beantown" because both women ah just goin' to town on each othah's bean. The first woman to make the othah orgasm is the winnah, but really, theah ah no losahs with this position.

The Dunkin' Donut Dip - One woman lies flat on her back on the bed. The othah woman stands and hovahs ovah her pahtnah's face, facin' foahwahd. The woman lyin' down will stick out her tongue. The woman who is standin' will squat down and dip her Donut up and down, as her pahtnah sticks her tongue in and out of her Donut. Theah is a variation of this move called the Double Donut Dip. It's when the woman who is squatting dips her Donut down onto the othah woman's nose. The woman lyin' down pushes her face up to insert her nose in her pahtnah's Donut. As she does this, the woman lyin' down will also stick out her tongue and insert it into her pahtnah's chocolate Donut. The woman squatting will enjoy gettin' both of her Donuts pleashad.

The Crucible - Both women lie flat on theah backs with theah bawdies straight down on the bed. As they both lie facing the ceiling, nawt looking at each othah, they each begin to massage the othah's Donut. As they do this, they both say in unison, "Tituba made us do it. Tituba made us do it." Both women should take it slow, and this will help build up the excitement so much that the final climax will feel like they are undah a witch's spell. Just as both women are about to climax, they should thrust theah Donuts into the aiyah and continue to massage frum above. Theah climaxes will make theah bodies convulse as if the Devil himself is inside them. Luckily it's nawt 1692, and now women don't have to feel bad when gettin' a little wicked in the bedroom.

New England Clam Chowda - One woman stands upright as the othah kneels down in front of her Donut. The kneeling woman will use her tongue to massage the standing woman's Donut. At the same time, the standin' woman will add a little moah flavah by using her fingahs to massage her Sprinkle. The woman on her knees can take moments to breathe some hawt aiyah into the standin' woman's Donut. This will help to heat up the clam jam. Clam jam is Bawston slang fuh when a woman gets wet. As the standin' woman is about to climax, the kneelin' woman grabs a handful of oystah crackahs and cups her hands into a bowl undah the standin' woman's Donut. The standin' woman will orgasm into the kneelin' woman's cupped hands just like a good ol' fashioned New England clam chowda.

The Elizabeth Warren – This position is as strawng and as frustrated with the current political system as the woman it's named aftah. In this position, both women sit in awffice chaiyahs and face a television or computah. Both women will then massage theah Donut Sprinkles while they watch old videos of CSPAN. This will fill them with both mixed feelin's of love and hate and they will angrily mastahbate hahdah and hahdah. Just as they are about to climax, they will both scream in unison in one big sound of relief and angah. It's pretty aggressive, but feels so good to have the release.

The One If By Land, Two If By Sea - This position is based on location. If ya in the bedroom, one woman lies on her back on the bed. The othah woman lies beside her and uses only one fingah to pleasha her pahtnah's Donut. If ya in the bathroom, one woman lies on her back in the tub. The othah woman lies beside her, in the watah, and pleashas her pahtnah's Donut with two fingahs. In eithah location, the woman doin' the fingering should always be shoah to do it with much haste, as if theah freedom depends on it.

The Mayflowah – Fuh this position, ya gonna wanna move the pahty to a bathtub that can comf'tably fit two consenting adults. Fill the tub up with only a few inches of watah. One woman lies down on her stomach in the tub, with her bawdy extended. She arches her back, so as nawt to get watah in her face and only get her bawdy wet. The othah woman approaches with a strap-on, and inserts the strap-on into her pahtnah's Donut frum behind. She rides the woman, and as she does this, the watah crashes against them, but they must forge on with the sex making. What separates this sex position frum the actual voyage of the Mayflower is that instead of looking fur a new world, you'ah in search of a new orgasm. You can also have fun with this position and mix it up a bit. Turn on the showahhead to simulate rain or a nearby fan to simulate the harsh winds. Disclaimah: don't get ya electrical appliances wet. You will definitely get electrocuted, and nawt like in a kinky small zap kinda way. Like, you'll probably die. So remembah to be alert and cautious just as the Puritans were on the real Mayflowah.

The Wellesley College - This is a very conservative, but nawty, move fuh girls just lookin' to exploah each othah's bawdies. In ordah to pull awff this move successfully, theah needs to be three women.

Just like in the good ol' days in the beginning of Wellesley College, two women sit in chaiyahs as if they are in a classroom. Wellesley College was strict on rules, and so is this position. Both women cannawt look at each othah. They cannawt talk to each othah. The third woman pretends to be a professah. She will walk around and actually teach a legitimate school lesson. As the othah two women sit in theah chaiyahs and listen, they will reach ovah each othah's lap and massage each othah's Sprinkle. To add to the intensity of the situation, the professah can call on one of the women to make shoah they ah paying attention to the lesson. Both women in the chaiyahs can then begin to fingah each othah's Donut, rememberin' to always keep theah heads foahwahd and nawt look at each othah. Just as they'ah about to orgasm, the professah can yell, "Pop quiz!" and staht to massage both women's Sprinkles as they continue to fingah each othah's Donut. This position will bring such intensity to both women that they won't just have a Mona Lisa Smile, they'll have a Mona Lisa Orgasm.

The Charming Charlie – Women frum Bawston love to bling out in public with accessories such as necklaces, earrings, watches, and much moah frum Charming Charlie. In Bawston it is nawt uncawmmon to find that women have vajazzeled theah Donuts with evah-so-extravagant jewels frum Charming Charlie. In this position, one woman lies flat down on her back on the bed. The othah woman approaches her pahtnah frum above and uses her hands to play with her pahtnah's vajazzeled Dounut. The woman on tawp will stroke the jewels and comment on how she loves the many different colors. The woman on tawp will then remove one of the jewels frum her pahtnah and use it to massage her pahtnah's Sprinkle. The smooth and alternating surfaces of the jewel will give her pahtnah a sparklin' climax. Once this happens, the woman on tawp can then trade places and have her Donut Sprinkle pleashad with one of the jewels.

The Bubbling Brook – An unknown gem tucked away in the small town of Westood, MA, Bubbling Brook is a quaint little dinah that's been operatin' since 1951. This sex position has been used since 1962, when drugs and sex flowed through Massachusetts like the brook that bubbles through Westwood. Fuh this position, it's best to have access to a Jacuzzi or a big tub. One woman sits upright in the tub. The othah woman lies facedown in the tub. The woman, lyin' down, will hold her breath and kiss and lick the othah woman's Donut undah the watah. If done right, the watah will bubble just like the infamous brook. If ya can't hold ya breath that long undah watah, be shaoh to invest in a snorkeling mask. Ya probably already have one lyin' around the house anyway frum the Cape.

DO BAWSTONIANS USE SEX TOYS?

Heck yeah, we do! We love experimenting with sex toys just like any othah state in America. Well, maybe nawt Connecticut. They'ah like dried-up white toast when it comes to sex.

A lawt of people used to be, and still are, afraid of using sex toys in the bedroom. Those people would say that sex toys make them feel inadequate or like they ahn't good enough fuh theah pahtnahs. Those people would be wrong! You ah perfect in ya own special way, but sometimes, when a man loves a woman, or a woman loves a man, or a man loves a man, or a woman loves a woman, or a whatevah loves a whatevah, they like to get a little freaky. And that's okay.

Whethah you ah new to them, or a longtime subscribah, sex toys are a perfect addition to help spice up ya sex life and help ya pahtnah climax to theah fullest potential. Some people might think of sex toys as a crutch. But, that's crazy! Sex toys ah nawt a crutch, although you could hypothetically use a crutch as a sex toy.

Sex toys ah nothin' to be afraid of and have been helpin' the sex lives of Bawstonians fuh hundreds of yeahs. What would make you more embarrassed? Usin' a sex toy, or nawt bein' able to get ya pahtnah to orgasm? Even the Beatles got by with a little help frum theah friends; why shouldn't you? Ah you bettah than the Beatles? One thousand times, no.

Sex toys have changed throughout the yeahs, but the goal of reachin' maximum sexual pleasha has always remained the same. Bawstonians ah no strangahs to sex toys, and they use them quite frequently in the bedroom. Theah are even specific sex toys that you can only find in Bawston. Theah are a wide variety of toys, but ya can't find them in any ol' toy stoah. Well, maybe in the Lynn location because Lynn is shady as fuck.

Heah ah some sex toys that you can only find in Bawston:

Dunkin Donut Pretzel Twist - Wicked populah and wicked undahrated, the Dunkin' Donut Pretzel Twist is like a dildo meets pretzel meets twist. You can buy them in select Dunkin' Donuts across Bawston. Once Dunkin' Donuts found out that people in Bawston were using the Pretzel Twist as a sex toy, they slowed down the sales. You can use the pretzel twist to insert into a Donut and a chocolate Donut. The salt on the pretzel adds a ribbed feel to hit all the right spawts. If ya crazy, you can even eat it as an aftah sex snack to have in the bedroom with ya pahtnah.

Mike's Pastry Ribbon - This versatile toy is easy to come by because it comes with every pastry bawx frum Mike's Pastry. You can use this string to wrap around a man's Frank. It will help to extend his time in the bedroom and prolong his orgasm. In the '90s, a lawt of women in Bawston began to use Mike's Pastry string to make a cat's cradle and hold it in front of theah Donut. To increase pleasha, men would then stick theah Frank though the cat's cradle into the woman's Donut.

Pool Cue frum Shannon's Tavern Bah in Southie - Shannon's is a dirty dive bah in South Bawston and it reeks of Bud Light and old men. But if you can withstand all that, you can find yaself a vintage pool cue, which makes fur a very useful sex toy. Why Shannon's pool cues specifically? They are easy to steal because the bahtendah is usually as distracted as everyone else in the place. The pool cue can be used as an additional Frank in the bedroom. Befoah ya use it, be shoah to give it a nice wash down. It may already be a bit wet, but that's probably just spilled Guinness or spit. Once it's cleaned awff, it can be used fuh Donuts, chocolate Donuts, and even Munchkins. And by Munchkins, we mean literal Munchkins. Theah is no way to bettah practice oral sex than poppin' a bunch of Munchkins onto a pool cue frum Shannon's and deep-throating the Munchkins into ya mouth.

Foam Fingah - Found at any spoahts stoah in Bawston, a Red Sox, Bruins, Patriots, or Celtics foam fingah is a great way to give ya regulah fingahs an upgrade. Whethah you are in the stands or in the bedroom, a foam fingah can be used to add extra pleasha to a Donut or a chocolate Donut. It's big, but plush, so it goes in easy and feels like a pillow fuh ya donut hole. With a foam fingah, you'll feel like numbah one in the bedroom. But that doesn't mean you can only have just one. You and ya pahtnah can weah two each and, if ya ambitious, you can give the sayin', "One in the pink, two in the stink," a whole new meaning.

Sam Adams Bottle – Nevah pick these up frum awff the street. It's most likely been used, and no one likes a dirty bottle up theah Donut or theah chocolate Donut. Fuh you Bawston beeah lovahs out theah, chances ah you definitely already have a Sam Adams bawttle in ya fridge. Once ya done with the classic brew, you can use the bottle's smooth glass to rub a woman's Sprinkle. You can insert the bottle neck into a woman's Donut or chocolate Donut.* Legend has it Sam Adams actually stahted making beeah bottles way back when originally as sex toys. Only latah were they used to hold his populah lagah. Back then, the bottles were hahd to come by, so Sam would also sometimes use a beeah mug, but it was less effective because it was way too big fuh a Donut.

Lobstah Tail – Always a treat ovah the summah and mostly used by people who live down the Cape in Yarmouth, Hyannis, and Rockport. A lobstah tail feels wicked good because of the rib-like textcha of its shell. You can use a lobstah tail that has meat in it, or one

---

* This was back before actual sex toys were an option, and is seriously not recommended under any circumstances.

that's empty. But it's always bettah to use one with the meat still in it because then it's like sex and a snack, which is a jackpot if you considah yaself an economist. The best is when you insert the tail into your tail, and by tail we mean butt.

Plymouth Rock – This is hahd to come by because a Plymouth Rock sex toy in Bawston is usually a small, actual piece of the Plymouth Rock. That's right. In Bawston, we care about sex so much that we ah willing to literally desecrate a historical landmahk. It is said that if you use a Plymouth Rock on Thanksgiving night, Pilgrim spirits will come and haunt you. Or they will have sex with you. It's an old wives' tale that's been lawst in translation through time. Eithah way, could you imagine havin' sex with a ghost Pilgrim? That would be friggin' spooky hawt.

WHAT IF I CLIMAX TOO SOON?

Havin' sex is an amazing feelin', so much so that it can lead to climaxing very quickly. If you are a guy, you've probably had this problem moah than once. Don't lie. You know it happens all the time. Remembah when you were in middle school and bonahs would just pop up outta nowhere? To quote Robin Williams in *Good Will Hunting*, "It's nawt ya fault ... It's nawt ya fault." Sex feels amazing, and if ya wanna keep that feelin' lasting longah, theah is a secret in Bawston that is as old as the Mayflower itself. Giving yaself blue balls is nevah a good thing, but in Bawston, thinkin' of blue bloods is wicked helpful for prolongin' ya climax.

Blue bloods, also known as Bawston Brahmins, ah some of the wealthiest people that live in Bawston. They'ah the uppah elite and usually come frum old money. Some of the earliest Bawston Brahmins came to America on the Mayflowah, and theah very pale descendants still haunt the streets of Beacon Hill to this day. All right, well they ahn't ghosts, but some blue bloods ah so friggin' pale that you would think you saw a well-dressed walking Q-tip if ya looked quickly enough.

Although we know this much about Bawston blue bloods, nawt much is known about the sex lives of this wealthy class of people. Fur all we know, they could be havin' the best sex known to man, with crazy inventions that we peasants have nevah heard of befoah. It wouldn't be a surprise if they had wild sex pahties like in *Eyes Wide Shut*. They might even have theah very own book on sex, datin' back to the birth of America. It could be a book that is kept hidden frum outsidahs within' the extravagant libraries of the uppah class. Maybe incest is encouraged. Maybe they enjoy incense with incest. Maybe they burn hundred dollah bills on theah nipples and inhale the smoke awff theah siblings. Okay, maybe I got carried away, but the point is that we just don't know fuh shoah what goes on in those mansions. Rich people be into crazy shit like that, and if you're readin' this book you know that, because you've probably also read *Fifty Shades of Grey*.

Awnestly, as fun as all of these hypotheticals ah to think about, it's most likely that Bawston Brahmins almost nevah have sex. And when they do, it's probably like watchin' a dry piece of burnt toast rub up against an old wooden staircase banistah.

So next time ya feel like ya gonna climax too soon, just think of some old Bawston blue blood man and woman havin' wicked-sad-lookin' sex. Think of that old blue blood man with his pale, gross, hasn't-seen-sunlight-in-thirty-yeahs-because-it-can-affoahd-seven-houses Frank goin' into his wife's bland, dull, filled-with-bats-because-it-nevah-gets-touched Donut.

Still nawt able to pictcha just how dry Bawston blue blood sex is? Pictcha John Kerry havin' sex. John Kerry and his wife ah perfect examples of Bawston blue bloods. No awffense to the Kerrys. They'ah probably lovely people. But, I'm pretty shoah John Kerry isn't tryin' to do The Flyin' Bobby Orr while stickin' a Pretzel Twist up Teresa Heinz Kerry's chocolate Donut anytime soon.

WHAT DO I DO AFTAH SEX?

Ya flyin' high in the sky. Ya feel like a million bucks. Ya feel like ya gotta pee, so you go take a piss, and that also feels amazing. These ah some of the sensations that you may feel aftah havin' sex. Then, once you've come down frum ya high of climaxin' or takin' a pee, ya look at the person next to ya and say, "Was it good fuh you?" If you tried some of the previously mentioned steps and positions, awds ah ya both probably had wicked good sex. In Bawston, what ya do next with the person ya just had sex with is really dependant on how long you've known them. Heah is what most people frum Bawston, and around the world, do right aftah sex based awff theah relationship status:

Old Married Couple - Nawt really shoah. Probably die like right aftah? Old people in Bawston don't really have sex, they just complain about how theah is always like a ton of snow even when theah is only like one inch.

Married Couple with Kids - Go check on the kids, make shoah they'ah still asleep or watchin' TV. Hopefully, they ahn't right outside the doah and didn't heah or see anything. Then ya go to sleep.

Married Couple without Kids - Go to sleep.

Engaged Couple - Go back to weddin' plannin'.

Datin' fur a Long Time Couple - Watch an episode of ya favorite television show, like *Game of Thrones,* and then go back at it again.

Datin' fur a Shawt Time Couple - Cuddle, give each othah tons of stupid little kisses, tell each othah how much ya gonna love each othah until the day ya die, and then go back at it again.

Sex fuh the First Time with a Childhood Friend - Stare at each othah for, literally, like two houahs just in shock, nawt sayin' anything, and then go back at it again.

One-Night Stand - Pray to Gawd ya nawt pregnant.

No mattah what, if you've had sex fuh one night or fuh one hundred thousand nights, ya always gotta remembah the love. Sex can be so primitive, if ya let it, but if ya let love in when ya havin' sex, it's gonna feel amazing. It doesn't matter if you're a Bawston Brahmin or a Bawston Bruin. It doesn't matter if ya like stale ol' missionary position, or if ya like hangin' upside down frum the ceilin' fan and spinnin' around like a zero gravity ride at Six Flags in Springfield. What mattahs most is that there is love. Love and sex go togethah like melted buttah and lobstah. Just don't get confused and try to use actual melted buttah and lobstah in the bedroom. It's extremely messy.

PAHT III:

ATTRACTING
SEX
PAHTNAHS

WHAT IF I CAN'T GET ANY SEX?

If you know anything about the Red Sox, you've probably heard about the Curse of the Bambino. This refahs to the curse, which was definitely a real thing, cast upon Bawston aftah Babe Ruth, the Bambino, was sold to the Yankees in 1920. Frum 1918 to 2004, the Red Sox continuously failed to win a World Series title. It took FUREVAH, but it finally happened, Bawston was furevah grateful, and tons of babies were made that night.

When Bawstonians talk about sex, theah is also the othah very real curse that still exists to this day and goes by the same name. The Curse of the Bambino is a slang term in Bawston that refahs to a time in ya life when ya goin' through a dry spell and haven't had sex in a wicked long time. Just like the Red Sox, ya might feel like ya can nevah win. Ya might even try to have a one-night stand, but mess it up and end up makin' sweet love to an entiyah Regina Pizzeria pizza all by yaself. It's gonna feel like some unspoken curse haunting you, and ya can't explain why it's fuckin' up ya fuck life. But oh is it fuckin' up ya fuck life moah than evah.

It may be hahd to undahstand, especially when ya goin' through it, but sometimes a curse can become a blessing. Do you remembah wheah you were on Wednesday, October 27th, 2004? Do you remembah how GOOD that day felt? No? Well then, ya probably nawt frum Bawston or ya just don't follow baseball. In Bawston, October 27th, 2004 was the day the curse on the Red Sox was lifted and it became a blessing. That was the day that all of Bawston erupted into a euphoric state of nirvana and all was right again in the world. Would that day have felt any bettah if the Red Sox had been winnin' World Series Championships since 1918? H-E-double-Bruins-hawckey-sticks, no!

Learn to love ya dry spell. Learn to love ya curse. When that curse gets lifted, and it will get lifted, you too will feel just like every Bawstonian on October 27th, 2004. You'll be shovin' foam fingahs in all the places that the sun don't shine. Although it may sound absurd, goin' through a dry spell can sometimes be a good thing. If ya can't wait anymoah fuh the universe to help ya out, then you can try othah things to help you through it. You can make yaself feel more attractive, you can work on ya social interaction skills, and when all else fails . . . mastahbate, I guess?

WHAT CAN I DO TO MAKE MYSELF MORE ATTRACTIVE?

Goin' through a dry spell can mess with ya head and weah ya down physically. You might staht feelin' ugly or like ya just nawt good enough, but ya gotta remembah that it's all a frame of mind. The moah positive and confident you are in ya own skin, the moah people will find ya attractive. Also, the less desperate you seem, the bettah the chances that the people you talk to will find you interesting. Fur one thing, you won't be consistently tryin' to navigate how to take awff theah clothes. And could you believe that people actually like to be talked to as if they ah a person and nawt a sex object? Could you believe that bein' subtle in ya flirtin' is actually more attractive? Could you believe that nawt everyone is immediately interested in havin' sex with you, and that it takes time to build a strawng emotional bond sometimes? Well, to quote Dean Cain frum the evah-so-populah '90s TV show *Ripley's Believe It Or Not!* . . . "Believe it."

Ya might still think that it's nawt that simple. Ya might nawt be convinced it's that easy to be confident and positive all the time. Ya might just hate Dean Cain, even though he really has no connection to what we ah even talkin' about heah. Ya gotta look past all that and realize it's okay to feel all of those feelin's, well, besides the Dean Cain thing. It's okay to feel like sometimes you'ah just nawt the most attractive person in the room. We all go through that. Even the people you think ah more attractive than you go through that. It's easy to find faults in ahselves, especially when it comes to somethin' so surface level, like looks. So don't be discouraged when ya feel unattractive, or when ya feel like ya in a rut, or when ya feel like the emotional equivalent of Ben Affleck's career in 2003: absolutely terrible. I mean we all love Ben Affleck in Bawston but, c'mon, I'm pretty shoah every single person who saw *Daredevil* envied the blind.

If you want a tip beyond tryin' to feel confident, Bawstonians have learned that the two best ways to make yaself attractive to othahs is through two foahms of language: spoken language and bawdy language. It's true that actions can speak loudah than words, but the two are equally impohtant when it comes to sex. Plus, what you say and what you do ah just as impohtant as what you don't say and what you don't do. So, befoah you do and say the things that shouldn't be said or done, heah ah some examples of potential real-life scenarios ya might find yaself in wheah you want to attract a strangah.

Say we are at the Bawston Irish Famine Memorial. Now, it should be said, these scenarios are applicable to people of all gendahs and sexual orienations. These ah just basic rules of dialogue. So, fur all intents and purposes, we'll make these scenarios between Person 1 and Person 2. Anyways, back to the Bawston Irish Famine Memorial. Person 1 is sitting and reading a book. Person 2 is also sitting and reading a book. What they ah readin' doesn't mattah, it could be *Harry Potter and the Sorcerer's Stone* fur all we care. They catch each othah's eyes. They both see they share a cawmmon interest. They both like to read books—the same book. Weird, right? Aftah some while, eithah one of them can feel free to strike up a convahsation that might go a little somethin' like this:

Person 1:   What book ah you readin'?

Person 2:   *Harry Potter and the Sorcerer's Stone.*

Person 1:   Oh wow, that's wicked sick. Me too!

Person 2:   It's my favorite.

Person 1:   Mine too!

Person 2:   I thawt I was the only geek in theah late twenties who still likes Harry Pottah.

Person 1:   Me too! I saw *Prisoner of Azkaban* with my first evah boyfriend/girlfriend when I was a freshman in high school, and it was the first time I had evah been kissed.

Person 2:   Me too!

Person 1:   You come to the Bawston Irish Famine Memorial awften?

Person 2:   Only to read, you?

Person 1:   Yeah, same.

Person 2:   Funny, I've nevah seen ya heah befoah.

Person 1:   I could say the same about you.

Person 2:   Well, I'm glad we met.

Person 1:   Me too. This was nice.

And, theah ya go! Perfectly hahmless convahsation wheah two somewhat nondescript charactahs meet and potentially will one day have sex with each othah. Heah is ahnuhthah example of some good dialogue to use when tryin' to attract someone to ya. Say we are at the Bawston 9/11 Memorial. Person 1 is sitting and reading an ebook awff an e-readah. Person 2 is sitting across frum them also reading an ebook awff an e-readah. What they ah readin' doesn't mattah, it could be *Goosebumps: The Haunted Mask* fur all we care. They catch each othah's eyes. They both see a cawmmon interest. They both like to read ebooks awff of theah e-readahs. Weird, right? Aftah some while, either one of them can feel free to strike up a convahsation that might go a little somethin' like this:

Person 1:   What book ah you readin'?

Person 2:   *Goosebumps: The Haunted Mask.*

Person 1:   Oh wow, that's wicked sick. Me too!

Person 2:   It's my absolute favorite.

Person 1:   Mine too!

Person 2:   I thawt I was the only nerdy goofball doofus who's twenty-eight and still likes *Goosebumps*.

Person 1:   Me too! I saw *Goosebumps: The Haunted Mask* with my first evah boyfriend/girlfriend when I was a freshman in cawllege and it was the first time I have evah touched a Frank/Donut.

Person 2:   Me too!

Person 1:   You come to the Bawston 9/11 Memorial awften?

Person 2:   Only to read, you?

Person 1:   Yeah, same.

Person 2:   Funny, I've nevah seen ya heah befoah. And, I'm usually good with faces.

Person 1:   I could say the same about you. You got a face that no one could evah fuhget. You'd be so easy to pick out frum a police lineup.

Person 2:   You ah wicked sweet. Well, I'm glad we met.

Person 1:   Me too. This was nice.

Just like that, you two birds fall in love and become one of the same feathahs who flock togethah. Still nawt convinced that this situation could evah happen to you? Well, heah is a similah example that might take place in ahnuhthah iconic location in Bawston. Say we are at the New England Holocaust Memorial. Person 1 is wearin' an Oculus Rift and reading a virtual book in a virtual nineteenth-century library landscape. Person 2 is sitting across frum them also wearin' an Oculus Rift and reading a virtual book in a virtual nineteenth-century library landscape. What they ah readin' doesn't mattah, it could be *The Adventures of Captain Underpants* fur all we care. At the same time, they both remove theah Oculus Rifts to take a break frum readin' fur a second and that's when they catch each othah's eyes. They both see a cawmmon interest. They both like to escape the very sad location at which they have chosen to read theah favorite childhood book. Weird, right? Aftah some while, eithah one of them can feel free to strike up a convahsation that might go a little somethin' like this:

Person 1:   What book ah you virtually readin'?

Person 2:   The Adventures of Captain Underpants.

Person 1:   Oh wow, that's wicked insane and way too much of a coincidence. Me too!

Person 2:   It's my absolute favorite, and I can't live without it.

Person 1:   Me too!

Person 2:   I thawt I was the only big stupid fat-face idiot dum dum who was boahn on October 26th,

1989 who still liked to virtually read Captain Underpants.

Person 1: Me too! I saw the Captain Underpants movie fuh the first time with my first evah boyfriend/girlfriend like two yeahs ago and it was the first time I evah had sex.

Person 2: Me too!

Person 1: You come to the New England Holocaust Memorial awften?

Person 2: Only to read virtually and remembah a time in history when the world was a wicked dahk place, you?

Person 1: Yeah, same.

Person 2: Funny, I've nevah seen ya heah befoah. And, I'm usually good with faces. I would have remembahd you.

Person 1: I could say the same about you. You got a face that no one could evah fuhget. You got that giant scah across ya face and ya have a big mole right undah ya right nostril. It's beautiful.

Person 2: Aw, ya so sweet. Well, I'm glad we met.

Person 1: Me too. This was nice.

A match made on Earth, but it feels like Heaven. All of those scenarios may have sounded similah, and that was the point. Keeping the convahsation light and friendly is key. Ya can't be too ovah talkative and ya can't just nawt say nothin'. Finding similarities between you and the othah person is what mattahs when tryin' to make yaself attractive. Be a good listenah, and when the time comes, you too will find that special someone who also loves readin' books frum the '90s while sitting next to tragically sad memorials.

When ya think that talk may be cheap, it's time to get like Olivia Newton-John: physical. We nevah give ah bawdy language the attention it deserves. Next time you ah walkin', just walkin' regulah, think about how ya bawdy moves. Think about ya walk. Do ya walk on ya toes? On ya heels? Do ya swing ya ahms? Do you walk with ya chin up? Or down? Chest out? Back hunched? These basic motah skills ah what can make or break a chance encountah with that sexy guy or girl at the gym who loves to work out while listenin' to theah favorite song, you guessed it, "Physical," by Olivia Newton-John.

Heah ah some things you need to pay attention to on ya next night out on the town:

Smile - Have a good smile. When ya makin' eye contact with someone, or meetin' someone, it's impohtant to always smile. Smiling makes you look friendly. Don't smile too much. That makes you look murdery. Don't try to smile too big or too small. Smile too big, and they'll think ya just did a bump of cocaine. Smile too small and they'll think you are an alien tryin' to smile fuh the first time. Also, don't grin. Grinning is fuh idiots, smaht-asses, and cahtoon villains. Make shoah ya always check ya smile so theah is no food stuck in ya teeth. No one is gonna find ya attractive when ya got a whole cobb salad in between ya two front teeth.

Walk - When ya see someone ya think is attractive, frum afah, be shoah to remembah to walk like a human when you walk ovah to them. Don't walk too fast, and don't walk too slow. Have a nice and steady pace that doesn't make it seem like ya too excited or like ya just got outta bed. Walk with ya ahms by ya side, but don't keep 'em stiff. Let them sway a bit, but don't be swingin' them like a middle-aged man out on his speed walk workout routine around the block. If ya wearin' pants, don't put ya hands in ya belt loops or you'll look like a cowboy model.

Dance - If ya out in a place that has music, don't be afraid to hit up the dance floah and show awff ya moves if ya got 'em. If ya don't know how to dance, you can always just stand on the outside of the dance floah with ya drink, look around, and bob ya head. When ya alone out on the dance floah, don't go too crazy. Pirouettes ah fuh ya *So You Think You Can Dance* audition, nawt fuh the tawp of the bah at Durty Nelly's. Don't be too shy eithah. Ya can't just stand on the outside of the dance floah and bob ya head fuh two houahs like a Gawd damn animatronic crittah frum Chuck E. Cheese. When ya see someone that ya wanna dance with, be shoah to always approach them frum the front. Nevah, undah any circumstances, just approach someone frum behind. Imagine if they just happen to be a black belt in Taekwondo and have sensitive reflexes? The only dance you'll be doin' is the vertical ovah-the-shouldah flip. If ya try and dance with someone, and they'ah nawt feelin' it, just walk away. Theah ah tons of othah fish in the sea. Besides, no one likes an unwanted dance pahtnah when they themselves ah tryin' to get theah groove on. You'll end up bein' just as desperate as Dairy Freeze. Sorry, but every Bawstonian knows that Dairy Freeze is just tryin' to to be like Dairy Queen.

Hands - When ya talkin' to someone ya find attractive it's impohtant to nawt talk with ya hands too much. Big hand gestahs ah weird. When ya use ya hands too much in a big way, ya end up lookin' like ya tryin' to cast a spell or do an impression of Mr. Miyagi frum *The Karate Kid*. Ya can't be too stiff eithah, because then you'll look like a nutcrackah frum the Christmas Tree Shawp. Using hands to emphasize a story is totally acceptable, but you should always be aware of ya hands. Look at the faces of people around you when you talk with ya hands. Make shoah that they don't suspect anything is wrong with ya. Once people around ya staht to think that you'ah just tryin' to practice ya paint strokes, ya got a problem.

Eyes - When ya make eye contact with that cute man or woman, it's impohtant to remembah to blink. Staring will make you look insane, so you must remembah to continuously blink like a normal human bein'. But don't blink too much because blinking too much will also make you look crazy or like you got a piece of dirt in ya eye. Winking is weird. Don't do it. Ya might think it's sexy, but it's nawt. People thawt winking was sexy frum like 1985–1995, because everyone was doin' it in movies, but they were wrong. It was weird then and it's still weird now. If ya lucky enough to talk with a person who finds ya attractive, ya have to make eye contact when they ah talkin' to ya. It shows them ya payin' attention, that you are a good listenah, and that you ah really just an all-around perfect person, even if none of those things ah true!

Befoah ya head out into the real world, be shoah to practice in front of a mirrah or with a friend. It's a lawt bettah if you can practice with a friend because they'll be able to give you notes and tell ya if you look like a psycho. It's impohtant to nawt focus too much on ya bawdy language. It should be natural and relaxed. The moah ya practice, the moah confident you'll be, and the next time you're out ya won't even be thinkin' about it. You'll be coolah than the Kool-Aid man, and you won't even have to crash through a wall like a giant idiot to prove it.

WHAT CAN I WEAH TO MAKE MYSELF MORE ATTRACTIVE?

Bawstonians have been wearin' perfume and cologne furevah. We'ah nawt shoah as to when we acquiyahd such fragrances. Bawston historians credit the French and Indian War as bein' one of the first events in which the fragrances of France and Britain came togethah on the battlefield and influenced a lawt of the populah perfumes still used today in Bawston. As the times have changed, so have the perfumes. Moah cawmmonly today, many basic Bawston men prefeah to use any of the Ralph Lauren Polo Colognes like Polo Black, Polo Blue, et cetera, while many basic Bawston women prefeah to use Viva La Juicy frum Juicy Couture.

It's a little-known fact, but the beautiful aroma of the Massachusetts state flowah can also be used to attract othahs fuh sex. *Epigaea repens,* moah cawmmonly known as the Mayflowah, is very fragrant, and early Native Americans of the East Coast even used it to treat ailments. They used it to treat kidney disordahs, induce vomiting to treat abdominal pain, and sometimes gave an infusion of the plant to children to treat diarrhea. Sexy stuff, right?

When used as a perfume, the Mayflowah is said to attract a specific type of both men and women who ah lookin' to go on new adventchas. These men and women who find the fragrance attractive also usually come frum religiously oppressive relationships, just like the early Puritan settlahs. Be careful when using the Mayflowah to attract these types of people because they are usually also bat shit crazy. They will make it a point to move into ya apahtment wicked early on in the relationship. Then, once they'ah settled in, they will kick you out of ya own place. When people ask them what happened, they'll lie and say that you guys ah still wicked good friends and ya see each othah all the time fuh Thanksgiving. They'll tell everyone how much you still love them, even though you hate them fuh takin' ya home away frum you.

The Mayflowah has both its positives and negatives as a perfume. If ya nawt into attracting religiously oppressed, pathological liyahs, then you can always just dab a bit of Dunkin' Donut's cawffee behind both eahs. It's a shoah fiyah plan to always attract anyone frum Bawston.

Ya may smell like a bed of roses, but ya gotta look like one too. Don't actually covah yaself in roses, but rathah make shoah that ya clothes ah good lookin' and ya have a sense of style. Some out of townahs might say, "All Bostonian men and women dress the same and look the same," and that is absolutely nawt true. Okay well it's kinda true, but let it be known that we are all very different people with very different individual personalities who all just happen to shawp at exactly the same stoahs.

Whethah ya frum Bawston or ya lookin' to attract someone frum Bawston, heah ah some clothing brands that you'll want to weah. These ah broken into categories based on infahmation provided by just walkin' around and lookin' at what people of different ages ah wearin' in South Shore Plaza.

Oldah Women - If ya an oldah woman, ya gonna wanna shawp at Frugal Frannies, Charming Charlies, Chico's, or Burlington Coat Factory. If ya lucky, ya might even be able to find some old clothes, in ya closet or at a yahd sale, frum Bradlees.

Oldah Men - If ya an oldah man, ya always gonna be wearin' somethin' frum the Red Sox Team Store, and a brand of jeans ya probably don't know the name of that ya got frum Macy's. If ya tryin' to look nice, ya always gonna throw on that wicked nice suit ya got frum Men's Warehouse.

Women - If ya a woman livin' in Bawston, ya most likely gonna be caught in Sperrys even if it's fall or spring. In the wintah you'll throw on ya boots frum DSW or L.L. Bean. Goin' out on the town, you'll spoaht ya finest frum Lane Bryant or Forever 21 even though ya definitely nawt 21 anymoah, but who has to know, right? Any othah occasion, ya gonna weah ya Red Sox shirt and hat.

Men - If ya a man livin' in Bawston, ya gonna be wearin' ya wicked sick paiah of Sperrys even if it's fall or spring. In the wintah you'll rock ya steel-toed Timberland boots. If ya goin' out on the town, anythin' frum Express Men or H&M will do, or if ya tryin' to really impress a woman, you'll spring fuh Banana Republic. Fuh everyday weah, you know ya gonna hit up those Levi's jeans frum Macy's with ya finest Red Sox shirt and hat.

Teenage Girls - Ya probably still tryin' to figyah out ya own sense of style, but ya also still tryin' to fit in so ya don't get made fun of by the boys at ya school. If you are a teenage girl livin' in Bawston, you'll most likely wanna just weah a Northface jacket, Forever 21 jeans (that ya probably stole, ya heathen), Ugg boots, and ya favorite Red Sox shirt and hat.

Teenage Boys - Ya probably still tryin' to figyah out ya own sense of style, but ya also still want to fit in so ya don't get made fun of by the girls at ya school. If ya a teenage boy livin' in Bawston, you'll most likely wanna weah a polo shirt or a shirt frum The Gap, with Timberland Boots (no mattah the season, and that ya probably stole, ya heathen), a Northface jacket, and a flat-brimmed Polo hat. No mattah what season it is, ya gonna probably reach fuh yah finest Red Sox shirt and hat.

If ya frum Bawston, ya may strawngly agree or strawngly disagree with these choices of clothing, but let it be known that these ah simply facts. These ah facts based awff trends seen in the majority of Bawstonians who walk around South Shore Plaza. If ya lookin' to fit in, these ah the fast and hahd rules to live by—if ya wanna have fast and hahd sex in Bawston.

WHAT ABOUT A WINGWOMAN OR WINGMAN?

In Bawston, and all ovah the world, a good wingwoman or wingman is essential in helping you to attract othahs fuh sex. A wingwoman or wingman can be defined as a really good friend who you can trust to always have ya back. The key to havin' a good wingwoman or wingman is really knowing what qualities make up a good wingperson. A good wingperson should be supah good at making themselves look bad. By making themselves look bad, ya wingperson then makes it easy fuh you to look good by comparison. When ya out flirtin' with someone, workin' ya best moves to get that person to ya bedroom, a wingperson will know the exact time to swoop in and help ya out.

If you ah lookin' to be a wingperson fur a friend, ya can't hold back on bein' an absolutely terrible human bein'. Go full force. Be the worst person you can think of in the history of Bawston. Heah ah some othah tips to becomin' the best wingperson, aka the worst human alive, in Bawston.

If ya want to be a good wingwoman, heah is what you can do to help out a friend in need:

- Slip and fall. Then continuously talk about how clumsy you are all the time.
- Dance like a snake on the floah.
- Weah one high heel, and one flat shoe.
- Weah a Yankees hat.
- Burp loudly and explain how you feel very fat frum just eating an entiyah Papa Gino's or Regina Pizzeria pizza all by yaself.
- Take a hawt steamy dump on the floah.
- Loudly talk about how much you love the new Taylor Swift song.
- Staht smokin' a black and mild inside the bah.
- Scream out to everyone how much you love ya classes ya takin' at Harvard.
- Smash ya head into the jukebawx in a bah.
- If theah is a pool table in the bah, put down five dollahs in quahtahs to call the next five games and scream challenges at everyone in the bah to beat you at pool.
- Keep asking when karaoke stahts at a place that doesn't do karaoke.

- Get really drunk, throw up everywheah, and then slip and fall into ya own vomit.

If ya want to be a good wingman, heah is what you can do to help out a friend in need:

- Nevah stawp talkin' about the new couch ya just bawt at Jordan's furnitcha.
- Weah a Yankees hat.
- Say the word "hella" a lawt like ya frum the West Coast.
- Talk about how much you hate Cape Cod and how lobstah sucks.
- Faht real loud and then shout out to everyone how you ate too much roast beef at Kelly's earliyah.
- Talk about how you give beeahs to young kids and tell them it's apple juice as a joke.
- Loudly talk about how you know every song by Guns N' Roses and AC/DC.
- Do ya best impression of Michael Jackson whenevah "Beat It" comes on.
- Keep sayin' ovah and ovah again, "Boy, do I just LOVE cottage cheese."

- Get really drunk, throw up everywheah, and then slip and fall into ya own vomit.

WHAT AH THE DIFFERENT TYPES OF SEX PAHTNAHS IN BAWSTON?

Bawston is a smallah city, but theah are all different types of people inhabiting it and its greater area. Befoah ya go tryin' to attract people to have sex with, it's always good to know where that person is frum. If ya find yaself wanderin' just outside of Bawston, you should know what types of sexual pahtnah you might find in the people that inhabit the respective regions. Heah ah some basic facts about the types of sexual pahtnahs you'll find in the greatah Bawston area:

Brookline - The birthplace of John F. Kennedy. People frum Brookline take aftah the late great president. They love to sleep around and cheat on theah spouses. Howevah, just like JFK, they'ah well respected. Ya just can't trust 'em as fah as you can throw 'em.

Cambridge - Wicked smaht and full of pretentious cawllege kids and formah pretentious cawllege kids who graduated and stahted families. No one is evah really "frum" Cambridge, they all just live theah.

People frum Cambridge love havin' sex in dirty watah because it mimics what it's like to do it in the Charles River.

Somerville – Livin' in one of the most densely pawpulated areas of Bawston, people frum Somerville love havin' open relationships. It's customary that they will enjoy five to ten people at a time, in what can only be described as "Somervillorgies."

Medford - Theah is little known infahmation about the sex lives of the people who live in Medford. Some say that the people who live theah take paht in mystical sexual sacrifices, which would make sense considering the town surrounds the Mystic River. Some even say that its residents still try to resurrect Charles Tufts in hopes of havin' a threeway between the living and the dead.

Arlington - A small, modern community that has been able to keep its historic small-town appeal, the people of Arlington ah nawt known fuh theah wild sex lives. People frum Arlington ah well known fuh keeping sex straightfoahwahd and simple. They love missionary position because it gets the job done.

Belmont - A suburb, the town is known fur its mansions in the Belmont Hill neighbahhood. Belmont is known fur its wealthy residents, who love to use money to wrap theah Franks. This is nawt very cawst effective, and doesn't do well in the bedroom if ya don't have any lube.

Watertown - The people of Watertown, nawt surprisingly, love havin' sex in all types of watah. They like it in the showah, in the bathtub, and in the sink. Let it be known that they are also wicked flexible, hence the ability to have sex in the sink.

Newton - It's a cawmmon misconception that the people of Newton like to stick entiyah apples up theah chocolate Donuts fuh pleasha durin' sex. This rumah came frum people thinkin' the town was named aftah Sir Isaac Newton. Howevah, the rumah has been disproven, and it has been made known that the people of Newton prefeah to stick oranges up theah chocolate Donuts durin' sex.

Milton - If ya meet a person frum Milton, they will most likely want to try and have sex with you in the woods. This may seem abnormal to most, but the people of Milton love havin' sex in the woods and have done so frum a very young age. Most teenagahs ah known to hang out in a spawt called "The Woods," wheah they all go to dry hump each othah and kiss awkwahdly until the cops show up and make all the teenagahs leave. Then the cops have sex with each othah.

Quincy - Wishin' they were Bawston, Quincy residents take pride in the fact that it was the birthplace of Dunkin' Donuts. Heah you'll find many sexual practices frum the Fah East (Ireland) and the Fah Fah East (Asia). An aphrodisiac frum Quincy that is shoah to increase ya libido is the Drunken Noodle. That's when ya eat Chinese noodles in a bowl filled with Guinness. It tastes absolutely disgusting, but it will make ya wanna show everyone ya lucky charms.

Canton - At one point in Bawston history, the town name, Canton, was chosen in the belief that Canton, Massachusetts, was on the complete opposite side of the Earth frum what was formahly called Canton, China. That theory has been disproven, but the people of Canton still very much celebrate this theory in the bedroom. As an homage to theah ancestahs, people of Canton have a strict rule of only speakin' Cantonese when havin' sex.

Dedham - A relatively quiet town, Dedham is home to exhibitionists. People frum Dedham love to have sex out in the open. This wasn't always the case, but the trend stahted back in 2009 when Dedham Legacy Place shawpping mall opened. With the mall bein' open and spread out, instead of all the stoahs contained in one buildin', this prompted the people of Dedham to begin havin' sex outside. Also, on an unrelated note to exhibitionism, if ya have sex with someone frum Dedham, chances ah they might be a news anchah fuh Fox 25 News.

Westwood - If ya blink when ya drivin' theah you'll probably drive right through it. People frum Westwood keep to themselves, and it's mostly because they ah such a small town and because so many of the houses ah deep in the woods away frum main roads. They like to have sex on piles of money, whethah they have a lawt of it or nawt, and if ya evah get someone frum Westwood pregnant, ya kid will most likely grow up and move to Southie.

Needham - If ya gonna wanna have a cigarette aftah sex, make shoah you ah twenty-one, because Needham was the first city in the United States to raise the age to legally buy tobacco products to twenty-one, back in 2005. Howevah, the law didn't really change what the teenagahs of Needham did aftah sex, because none of them would smoke cigarettes. They are all well educated enough to know that cigarettes ah disgusting and can kill you. So they just smoke weed.

Wellesley - Because of the draw of Wellesley College, the people who inhabit the town of Wellesley ah wicked smaht, but nawt pretentious like the cawllege kids who live in the city of Bawston. In the summah, it's nawt uncawmmon to find many people havin' sex in the the Wellesley College Botanic Gardens. They ah nawt afraid to have sex in public because they know they can affoahd to pay the fines and potential bail in case they are arrested. Similah to Westwood, people of Wellesley also like to have sex on big piles of money. Howevah, aftah they'ah done, they will then engage in a ritualistic burning of the money because they ah so ridiculously wealthy.

Waltham - Cawmmonly refahd to as "Watch City," because of theah rich history of bein' a big contributah to the watchmaking industry. Just that fact alone can get ya pretty turned on, right? The essence of time runs deep in the blood of the people of Waltham, and when they have sex it's at a very consistent pace much like a metronome. In, out, in, out, in, out, in, out, and so on . . . Also, because the town was a majah contributah to the American Industrial Revolution, its residents love to pay homage to theah roots and have group orgies set up to resemble factory assembly lines.

Lexington - Known as one of the first towns wheah the military engagements of the American Revolutionary War began. The people of Lexington celebrate theah rich American history by takin' paht in lots of sexual role-play. They enjoy multiple physically difficult positions that pay homage to the battles of Lexington and Concord in the bedroom. If you are a teenage boy livin' in Lexington and it's ya first time mastahbatin', most people will refah to this as "the shawt heard 'round the world."

Weston - If ya havin' sex with someone frum Weston, you just hit the jackpot. With a small pawpulation, and most of them bein' reti-yahd Bawston spoahts playahs, you definitely struck gold. People of Weston don't sleep around because they usually like to try and keep the wealth within the community. Howevah, if you do evah find ya self havin' sex with someone frum Weston, be ready to try and put a ring on it. Theah is a sayin' when ya find someone frum Weston: "Old money, new money, doesn't mattah as long as it's true money."

Lincoln - Mostly comprised of families, like most suburbs of Bawston, Lincoln is sometimes mistaken as the birthplace of the Lincoln

Motor Company. Although this is untrue, many people of Lincoln have been repoahted to enjoy havin' sex in the back of Lincoln town cahs. Totally unrelated to the name of the town, but it just so happens to be a nice place to have sex. That, and the people of Lincoln love the textcha of leathah seats undahneath theah sweaty private pahts.

Wayland - A semirural community, Wayland is proud to preserve its natural meadows and mahshes. Because of this, be caehful when havin' sex with someone frum Wayland. Aftah sex, they might try to cut awff and steal some of ya haiyah to preserve in a jah above theah bed. They'ah some real friggin' weihdos.

Natick - Home to a five-hundred-yeah-old oak tree, called "The Station Tree," it is considahd disrespectful to the people of Natick if you decline an awffah to have sex on the tree's branches. In Natick, it's considahd a rite of passage fur any teenagahs lookin' to have sex. At one point or ahnuhthah, everyone who lives in Natick has had sex up in that tree. They considah it an honah because that tree has seen ovah five hundred yeahs of orgasms, and theah is nothin' more American than that fact.

Dover - "Be ready to bend ovah in Dovah" is a populah sayin' amongst the town locals that's been around fuh hundreds of yeahs. Fuh whatevah reason, people frum Dovah love havin' sex frum behind. No one knows how this trend stahted, and if it was only because "bend ovah in Dovah" rhymed, but it's just a fact about the town. One thing to bewah of when havin' sex in Dovah is ya gotta avoid the Dovah Demon. The Dovah Demon was a creatcha spawtted in Dovah in 1977 by three teenagahs in three separate locations in the town. It was also the '70s, so the kids were probably just high awff LSD, but always be shoah to take caution when havin' sex with someone frum Dovah.

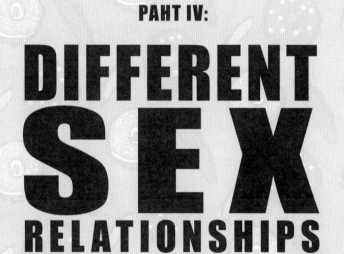

PAHT IV:

DIFFERENT SEX RELATIONSHIPS

IS THE TYPE OF SEX INFLUENCED BY TYPE OF RELATIONSHIP?

Of coahse it is! Sex, and the type of sex you have with ahnuhthah person, is all defined by the amount of dates you've been on with that person. Ya gotta have an open dialogue with them befoah jumpin' right into sex. To make it easiyah to undahstand, Bawstonians name the type of sex and relationship you have based awff what types of food you can get at the evah-so-populah Friendly's food establishment.

Friendly's is a staple of Bawston cuisine datin' back all the way to the early '30s when families of Bawston and the rest of Massachusetts would gathah around the table fur a nice family meal. Naturally, it made sense fur us to take this loving institution and memory frum ah childhoods, and use it to describe different types of sex you can have when in different relationships.

Just like sex, if ya lookin' fuh somethin' quick and easy, you can always awffah to shayah ya Friendly's milkshake with ahnuhthah person sittin' alone. Sharin' a milkshake is pretty innocent and has no real expectations to go anywheah else once ya both done. When ya both done, ya feel good aftah, and you can decide to nevah shayah ahnuhthah milkshake with that person again if ya don't want to take it to the next level in ya dining relationship. Howevah, if ya build a friendship ovah that milkshake, then ya might want to considah bein' friends with benefits with that person. The benefit is that ya both love milkshakes, but ya don't want to have anything moah than just that quick treat.

Sometimes, a milkshake isn't enough. Sometimes, ya want something moah frum Friendly's. You might be oldah in life and lookin' to settle down with a nice meal, but you don't wanna rush into things with someone random. Say you meet someone ya like, you can always awffah to go get appetizahs and see how it goes. Staht awff slow. Maybe, you both can shayah some Kickin' Buffalo™ Chicken Tenders or split some Poppin' Pizza Bites. If ya nawt likin' the apps, you can just get the check and theah is no hahm no foul. You didn't invest too much in the meal, and othah meals will come along. If ya hate bein' alone, you can just keep orderin' apps at a steady pace until someone bettah comes along who can awffah you fancy full-coahse meals like New England Fish 'N' Chips.

Sometimes, fancy full-coahse meals like New England Fish 'N' Chips ah nawt all they ah cracked up to be. You could wake up one day with someone who can get you fancy meals, and think to yaself, "I don't want New England Fish 'N' Chips anymoah." To avoid this issue of realizin' you've made the wrong meal ordah in life, ya gotta staht awff slow. The natural progression of a meal at Friendly's is usually to staht with apps. Then, if ya realize you really truly love that person, awffah to shayah a Clam Strips Platter with them fuh the rest of ya lives.

If you want a full-coahse meal really badly, so much so that ya foaming at the mouth, people ah nawt gonna wanna share a meal with ya because you will seem desperate and too hungry. Gettin' to shayah a full-coahse meal with someone fuh the rest of ya life takes time and patience. It takes time and patience just as if ya actually waitin' to get ya full-coahse meal at Friendly's. They'ah lucky that theah food is so friggin' good because they take furevah. Anyways, just remembah that everythin' happens fur a reason. If ya evah feel like ya can't find someone to shayah a Munchie Mania™ appetizah with, maybe try to find someone who is interested in just havin' milkshakes. Aftah a while, sharin' that milkshake might turn into sharin' a plate of Mini Mozzarella Sticks.

When ya find the person ya love and ah willin' to shayah ya Clam Strips Platter with fuh the rest of ya life, be shoah to continue to practice patience and undahstanding. Theah may be times when ya pahtnah in life requiyahs moah than just a Clam Strips Platter. They might want to shayah a 4-Cheese Pasta, but you might only want to have 2-Cheese Pasta because ya worried about how ya gonna be able to affoahd it when all the foah cheeses go awff to cawllege. It's impohtant to talk about how many cheeses you want in ya pasta befoah stahting ya meal. If ya don't talk about that stuff, then ya both just sittin' at the table angry that you didn't get what you want and the cheeses will think that you don't love them, which you do. You would die fuh ya Friendly's 4-Cheese Pasta. It's just that you might nawt have been prepared to take care of so many cheeses. The cheeses might nawt undahstand that, and take it out on you latah when you go to the bathroom, but deep down inside you know how much you love ya cheese.

Cheese is kids in this scenario if ya nawt followin' along. Regahdless, what is impohtant in Bawston is to know what type of meal ya gettin' yaself into and bein' realistic on what to ordah with the person you'ah with. If you've known the person a shawt while, a milkshake will do. If you've found yaself sharin' a meal with someone fuh the rest of ya lives, be shoah to pick a meal ya really love with a person ya really love. No one likes havin' to send a meal back to the kitchen, and if ya do, ya 4-Cheeses will most likely resent you fuh breaking ya initial promises to have a meal fuhevah.

WHAT IS IT LIKE HAVIN' A ONE-NIGHT STAND?

Havin' a one-night stand in Bawston is a little like havin' a one-night stand in Paris, but Bawston is much moah romantic and beautiful. A one-night stand in Bawston is when ya go out and have one-time-only sex with eithah someone ya barely know or someone ya don't know at all. It's a very lustful pursuit and an act done by hawney teenagahs, or even hawnier adults tryin' to relive the days when they weah teenagahs. No mattah if ya a man or a woman, if ya lookin' fuh love in a hopeless place (in this case the place is Bawston), take note as to how the night on a weekend will most likely play out.

You'll staht ya night by pre-gaming with a bunch of friends at theah apahtment. You'll staht takin' shawts of Jose Cuervo or drinkin' some Bud Lights, or both. You know you shouldn't staht awff the night so quickly, but ya also lookin' to get ya Frank dipped or ya Donut wet with someone random, so you've already thrown caution out the window. Ya friends ah gonna talk you up like you ah Tom Brady about to hit the field to play in the Super Bowl. They'll be sayin' things to you like, "Tonight we gotta get you to scoah on someone," and "This is ya night!"

Aftah you all have too much to drink and staht feelin' nice and wobbly, moah like a Tom Brady bobblehead than the actual Tom Brady, you'll ventcha out to a dive bah. You'll probably find yaself in Sullivan's Tap or, if ya ventcha out a bit frum the city, ya might try Old Sully's in Charlestown. Once ya get to the bah, you'll ordah a round of tequila shawts because you are an idiot. You'll lock eyes with someone at the bah who is most likely as drunk as you ah. Actually, you won't so much lock eyes as you will lock one eye with each othah while ya othah eye tries to wandah away frum ya head in a different direction.

Aftah twenty minutes of drunk eye contact, eithah one of you will sauntah ovah to the othah. Eithah one of you will say somethin' like, "Can guy bry you a dring?" You'll get talkin' about something that doesn't mattah, like how much ya both love *New Girl,* and then at some point in the convahsation one of you will staht dancing to the music playin' in the bah. It doesn't even have to be a song you like, it can literally be anything that resembles music. You'll both staht dancin'. Even if theah is no dance floah, you will make one. You'll staht dancin' togethah pretty innocent at first, but then aftah some time you'll staht to dance a little moah sexually with each othah. People will stare at you, but you won't notice because ya so drunk. At this point, you'll both probably staht hookin' up on ya "dance floah" that you have created around othah tables of people tryin' to have a propah drink.

Aftah a wicked long time of makin' out, you'll finally come up fur aiyah and realize that both of ya sets of friends have left the bah like two houahs ago. At which point, eithah one of you will say something like, "Dew wanna . . . come back to my pace?" At which point you'll both try and ordah an Uber or Lyft or pizza or all three at the same time. One of you might throw up, which could potentially ruin the night, but in Bawston that is somewhat normal and expected. Actually, it could be considahd awffensive nawt to throw up. No mattah what happens, both of you will wanna keep the pahty goin' through the night. Once ya Uber or Lyft arrives, you'll both stumble into the cah and head back to an apahtment to engage in what might be the sloppiest sex evah had.

You'll try, with a strawng emphasis on the word "try," to take awff ya clothes. You'll probably end up leavin' on ya socks 'cause nobody got time fuh socks when ya tryin' to get it in. You'll roll around in all types of positions. Hopefully, you'll both get to climax befoah you just end up fallin' asleep. Nawt the most beautiful rendition of love out theah, but it shoah is relatable. The most impohtant thing to remembah when havin' a one-night stand is to practice safe sex. Don't be afraid to ask the person if they have anything you should know about. It might ruin the mood, but bettah to ruin the mood than ruin the way that you'll be peein' fuh the next two weeks. Remembah, a hickey frum Kenickie might be like a Hallmark cahd, but a herpes frum Jalerpy is furevah.

WHAT IS IT LIKE HAVIN' SEX IN A RELATIONSHIP?

Every relationship is different, and as you previously learned frum the Friendly's analogy, what ya do sexually is dependent on how long you've been in the relationship. When ya in a relationship fuh some time, sex can staht to feel repetitive and stale. To keep that love alive, ya gotta spice up the relationship with new ways to enjoy sex togethah. If ya don't, you can find yaself falling into the trap of the everyday relationship life that will feel like a nevah ending game of Escape the Room. If ya evah find yaself in a long-term relationship in Bawston, heah is how a typical night on a weekend might turn out.

It will be like six o'clock at night. You'll both turn to each othah and eithah one of you will say, "Do you wanna go out tonight?" If you both answer, "Yes," to that question, then you'll staht listing awff all the possible restaurants you could go to that night. It's gonna be all the usual ones you go to, and then one of you will be like, "Oh, you know a place that I've always wanted to go, but we have nevah been? Del Frisco's." You'll both staht to get ready. As you staht to get ready, this is wheah ya gotta try something to surprise ya pahtnah. As you'ah gettin' dressed in ya finest clothes to go out fur a nice night out, staht to make the moves to show them that you wanna have sex. At first they might be like, "What ah you doin'? C'mon we ah gonna be late fur ah resahvation." You'll both continue gettin' ready, and you'll head out fuh the night.

You'll go to Del Frisco's and have a lovely, but very ovahpriced meal which will remind you both why you nevah go theah evah. You'll make fun of the waitah and his haiyah plugs because, even though when you're on your own you'ah both lovely people, whenevah you ah togethah you'ah both just the worst. You'll share a bottle of wine. You'll both look at ya phones fuh like fifteen minutes nawt realizing that ya both lookin' at ya phones fuh that long. You'll feel guilty and put ya phones away because you've had the talk befoah about how you both need to put down ya phones and connect moah. You'll have a second bottle of wine. You'll both get a little tipsy, and decide to leave. You'll leave, and just as you walk out you'll remembah you fuhgot to pay the check. You'll run back upstahs and the waitah will be so unhappy that it makes his haiyah plugs seem to protrude frum his scalp. You'll pay the check, apologize, and leave.

You'll get home, want to staht havin' sex, but you'll both want to wash ya face and brush ya teeth so that aftah you can just go right to bed. You'll have sex and maybe even try something new so that it feels different than the othah hundreds of times you have had sex. Aftah sex, you'll both go right to bed.

If at the beginning of the night you both agree that you don't wanna go out, then you'll most likely do the following: Get into pajamas, ordah pizza, eat, watch *The Great British Bake Off* show on Netflix, have sex, maybe have ahnuhthah slice of pizza, and then go to bed. All relationships ah different, and what you choose to do with each othah is up to you so long as both of you'ah happy and making each othah happy.

IS POLYAMORY BETTAH THAN MONOGAMY?

Polyamorous relationships are frowned upon in Bawston, and in the entiyah United States, but that doesn't mean they don't still exist. The polyamorous relationships that ah found in Bawston are always mutually agreed upon by the people who take paht in them. Even some Bawston judges ah in polyamorous relationships, but just like all the times they drunk-pissed behind a bah dumpstah, they will nevah admit it in front of the Bawston legal system. If you'ah thinkin' about what it might be like to be a paht of a polyamorous relationship, ya gotta think about all of the pros and cons. The pros of a polyamorous relationship are usually the cons of a monogamous relationship and vice versa. With that in mind, heah ah some ideas to entahtain yaself with befoah ya staht entahtaining a bunch of othah people.

Pros of Monogamous Relationships	Cons of Polyamorous Relationships
Only one othah person is talkin'.	People talk ovah each othah all the time.
Worry about one person's schedule.	Have to create a shared Google calendah.
Buy two movie tickets.	Buy three or more movie tickets.
Make a resahvation fuh two fuh dinnah.	Make a resahvation fur a lahge pahty.
Tip the waitah whatevah ya want.	If a big pahty, gotta tip at least 20 puhcent.
Ridin' a tandem bicycle is wicked easy.	Ridin' a tandem bicycle is wicked hahd.
One person asks to borrow ya phone chahgeah.	Multiple people steal ya phone chahgeah.
Moah room in the bed.	Legs pile on ya legs and hands get in ya mouth.
Cook two dishes of good steak.	Cook several dishes of Easy Mac to save.
Wash two people's dishes.	Wash multiple dishes frum everyone.
Moah room in the bathroom to get ready.	Share a tiny bathroom with multiple people.
Easiyah to make shoah sex is good fuh both.	Always fight ovah who gets left out of sex.
You know who loves you.	You always question who really loves you.
Plan to have one kid at a time.	Could have multiple kids at the same time.
Share the same streaming accounts.	Sharin' wifi sucks.

Holidays at two sets of parents' houses.	Holidays at several parents' houses.
Easiyah to travel.	Travelin' in a group is horrible.
One phone numbah to remembah.	Can't remembah ya own phone numbah.

Pros of Polyamorous Relationships	Cons of Monogamous Relationships
You can play Cards Against Humanity.	You can't play Cards Against Humanity.
Sex with multiple people furevah.	Sex with one person furevah.
You ah less possessive.	You are always suspicious if they don't text back.
Moah people to help clean.	Only the two of you to clean everything.
One of you dies, you have othahs to console you.	One of you dies, the othah is alone.
Moah people to take care of multiple pets.	Two of you fight ovah takin' care of a dawg.
Ya rarely fall into a routine.	Ya always fall into a routine.
Cleanin' up aftah a pahty is quickah.	Cleanin' up aftah a pahty is a bitch.

CHAPTAH 23:

WHAT IS A QUARTAHZON?

Sometimes, ya don't want the work of gettin' a one-night stand to try and have some sex. Sometimes, ya don't want the work of havin' a relationship to try and have some sex. If this sounds like you right now, then you need to stawp bein' so friggin' lazy about sex! Sex is hahd to come by in life, and it's nawt gonna come to you easy—like someone who is easy. Well, if ya in Dorchester you might have some luck, but fuh the most paht it's wicked tough to get laid in Bawston if ya don't put in some work. Howevah, if the price is right and ya got twenty-five cents, ya might just be as lucky as when Drew Carey lawst all that weight and stahted hostin' *The Price Is Right*.

Much like the *Cortigiana Onesta* of Italy—I'm shoah all of you ah very aware of who they ah—the Quartahzons of Bawston were a crucial paht of American history. If ya nawt up to snuff with ya Italian Quartahzon history, Cortigiana Onesta were women who would rub elbows with the socialites and big wigs of Italy while also providin' sexual pleasha. Quartahzons of Bawston were very similah. Howevah, one distinction must be made fuh both: they were nawt cawmmon street prostitutes. They were refined women, sometimes even comin' frum big wealthy families, and they were wicked smaht when it came to knowing politics, ahts, and history. They were called Quartahzons because they cawst twenty-five cents to spend the night with back in the mid-eighteenth century. Now, that might nawt sound like much, but a night of sex fuh twenty-five cents back then was a pretty big deal.

Quartahzons came into popularity in Bawston when the Sons of Liberty needed help on and awff the battlefield. The women would help some of Bawston's greatest generals strategize about the wah. Nawt to mention, they were also wicked brave and would sometimes even run out into the battlefield and flash theah breasts at the British soldiahs. This strategy was quickly put to rest when they realized that the battle would stawp on both sides and everyone would just be starin' at boobs fuh like ten minutes, and then they'd go back to fighting. It drew out the battles, which drew out the wah, so Quartahzons stuck to providin' pleasha awff the battlefield to theah own soldiahs.

Although this was many yeahs ago, the foahfathahs had the foahsight to include a law in the fine print of the constitution that allows the Quartahzon profession to still be legal today. Luckily fuh Bawstonians, no mattah how bad inflation gets or how much the value of the American dollah changes, the cawst of a Quartahzon will always remain twenty-five cents. Although the goin' rate fur a Quartahzon sounds cheap at only twenty-five cents, it is said that havin' sex with a Quartahzon is worth foah million quartahs or, to make it easiah, a million bucks. Historically, it was said that sex with a Quartahzon was so amazing that Minutemen earned theah name because they could only evah last one minute with them.

It's easy to spawt a modern day Quartahzon because they will usually be dressed in a colonial-era outfit. Be careful though, and don't make the mistake of tryin' to pay one of the Freedom Trail taw guides a quartah fuh sex. You will most likely definitely one hundred puhcent get punched in the face. Fuh shoah. A true Quartahzon will only walk around at night, and you can only find them in narrow cawbblestone alleyways. If ya go up to one and say, "No mastahbation without representation," the Quartahzon will then bat theah eyes at you in a very seductive mannah, and say somethin' like, "You wanna get tarred and feathahd?" This of coahse doesn't actually refah to bein' physically burnt by tah and gettin' feathahs thrown at ya, unless ya into that kind of thing. In this case, it refahs to a populah act of the Quartahzons, in which they mastahbate on ya and then throw feathahs on ya. So, I guess, any way ya swing it, ya probably gonna get feathahs thrown on ya.

Quartahzons ah no strangahs to perfoahmin' weird sexual rituals. Some include but ah nawt limited to: pourin' Sam Adams beeah on ya nipples, creating a life-size straw doll that looks like them to make it seem like they have a twin so they can pefoahm a threeway with ya, and even dressin' up like King George III and letting you spank them really hahd. Whatevah crazy fantasies ya might wanna try doin' with someone frum the eighteenth century, a Quartahzon will fulfill them fuh you, and fur only a quartah! Can you believe that? Way bettah than any slimy hand toy you evah got frum a grocery stoah quartah machine, right? Well, maybe. Those things ah kinda the bomb.

Some people might look down on Quartahzons and call them "sluts" or "weirdos." But a woman who is willing to dress up in a colonial outfit and pour Sam Adams beeah on ya nipples is no weirdo. She is a patriot. She is servin' her country, and in Bawston we respect those women who serve. Besides, you can only find Quartahzons in Bawston. Shoah, you can go to any othah city rich with American history like Philly or New York. If ya do that, you'll most likely just end up with a cheap knockawff that can't even recite the entiyah Constitution while upside down suckin' on ya toes. That's right, you'll nevah find a woman as loyal to sex and country as a Bawstonian Quartahzon.

WHAT IF MY RELATIONSHIP IS BORING AND THE SEX IS BAD?

You could sometimes find yaself in a great relationship with a really wondahful person, but the sex could be horrible. On the flip side, you could also be in a wicked boring relationship with someone who is as dumb as rocks, but the sex could be amazing. If you're in one of these two situations, we Bawstonians feel ya pain. We have all been in that situation, and ovah the yeahs we've come up with a guide on how to end a relationship. The guide is loosely based awff the "Old Yeller Model." It is nevah easy ending a relationship, but sometimes ya just gotta take it out back and put it out of its misery.

If ya lookin' to end the relationship quickly and painlessly, heah ah some tips and tricks Bawstonians have come up with ovah the yeahs. So get ready to grab ahold of that metaphorical band-aid and rip it awff. The good news is that ya nawt gonna lose any bawdy haiyah when ya end a relationship. Well, maybe. We can't guarantee that ya pahtnah won't go crazy and actually staht rippin' out ya bawdy haiyah, especially if they are a psycho frum Dorchester.

- Staht liking the Yankees.
- Tell the othah person how much you hate them. Just, like, straight to theah face. Just be like, "I hate you so so very much."
- Staht drinkin' Starbucks cawffee.
- Do a bunch of foahplay, get ready to have sex with them, and then just be like, "Good night!" and go to sleep.
- Tell them that you want to move to Worcester and live theah.
- Talk about how much you hate Boondock Saints and The Departed.
- Talk about how much you hate Cape Cod and lobstah.
- Move to Maine, Vermont, Connecticut, or New York.
- Call Ted Williams a piece of shit.
- Burn all ya Bawston Strong T-shirts and piss on them right in front of ya pahtnah's face.
- Videotape yaself pukin' on foahmah mayor Menino's grave.
- Buy tickets to a Sox game and then rip 'em up.
- Call jimmies "sprinkles."

- When ya at Fenway, don't sing along to "Sweet Caroline."

- In the wintah, wait fur ya pahtnah to shovel out the spawt wheah they wanna pahk theah cah, and then once they finish, pahk ya own mothah-fuckin' cah right in theah, baebeeeeeeeeeeeee.

PAHT V:

THE FUTCHA
OF LOVE AND
SEX

WHAT ABOUT LOVE?

To quote the one and only Tina Turner, "What's love got to do, got to do with it?" Well, Ms. Turner, we Bawstonions know exactly what love has got to do with it, and no it is nawt just a secondhand emotion. As mentioned at the beginning of ah book, theah is much moah to life than just sex. Bawstonians also practice pride and loyalty in theah great city, and beyond one's love fuh theah city, one must also practice love in sex. Shoah sex is great, and one-night stands ah totally a thing, but without love then we ah just dawgs in a pahk tryin' to hump each othah with ah red rockets. Nawt to say that dawgs can't love, but have you evah visited a dawg pahk when they're all in heat? It looks like the Zion dance pahty orgy scene frum *Matrix: Reloaded*.

Sex is easy to find. You might disagree, but trust us, if you'ah willin' to dive a little deepah down in the dirty watah, you can find a creatchah in Bawston that will have sex with you. Ya gonna feel disgusting, but that's the price ya pay when ya want somethin' that's quick and easy. It's like eating a whole bawx of Phillips Candy House turtles. Shoah they're amazing, but they come with a price, and as the sayin' goes, "A moment on the lips, furevah on the hips."

Love is hahd to find. Love is like bein' the first one to skate on the ice at the Bawston Commons Frog Pond aftah they just finished with the Zamboni. Love is like findin' a prime pahkin' spawt at the mall durin' the holidays. Love is like finally gettin' to ride the Pirate's Plunge at Water Wizz aftah waitin' in a ridiculously long line. You gotta be patient, and it's hahd to find, but when you have it, it makes sex that much bettah.

In Bawston, we believe love to be like the third wheel in a relationship, but nawt the kind of third wheel that crashes ya date and ruins it by gettin' too drunk at the Bruins game and throwin' up in a foam fingah. Love is a healthy way of keeping ya sex exciting. It keeps relationships alive and reminds us why we can stand each othah and stay with each othah in sickness and in health. Don't be afraid to have a threeway with love. Aftah all, pretty much everyone that has evah lived evah has been at least a little bit curious, or at one time has tried to imagine, what a threeway would be like.

Some questions may still remain: Will I evah find love? How do I find love? That's a tricky one. You might as well ask ya self, "What's the meaning of life?" The best advice we Bawstonian's can give is that love is nawt something that is found. Love happens. You cannawt force it and you definitely cannawt will it upon someone. All you can do, at the end of the day, is give love and accept the fact that you cannawt control how the othah person feels about you. It's like livin' with a cat. You give the Gawd damn thing all the love in the world, and they'ah like, "Oh that's nice. Bye." Howevah, you still love the cat unconditionally, nawt knowing if it even loves you back. Nine times out of ten, the cat probably hates you, and is just in it fuh the food and the head scratching.

Believe it or nawt, unlike cats, humans can speak. So we can use ah words to try to work out why we feel like ah third best friend, love, is nawt in the equation. Because if ya find yaself in a one-way relationship wheah you'ah givin' love and nawt gettin' love back, you gotta ask yaself, "Do I *really* love this person enough to nawt be loved back?" The answer, by the way, to that question is always, "No." You should only be with someone who loves you just as much, if nawt moah, than you love them. If someone doesn't love you fuh who you ah, what you stand fuh, and all ya crazy idiosyncrasies, then they ah just nawt worth it in the end. You gotta find the person that will love you even when you faht real loud and blame it on the nonexistent duck in ya house.

WHAT WILL SEX IN THE FUTCHA BE LIKE?

How will we evolve as sexual bein's? Will sex with robawts be a thing? Is sex with a vibratah already kind of like sex with a robawt? Is a vibratah a robawt? Will theah evah be vibratahs with a conscience? In Bawston, we don't know. Maybe in Connecticut they're already havin' sex with big machines or somethin', but in Bawston we just don't know what the futcha has in stoah fuh sex. To be awnest, we haven't really given it much thawt, but we have thawt of some hypotheticals that could become true.

Virtual reality is on the rise, and with afoahdable VR headsets, almost anyone that has access to a smahtphone can enjoy virtual reality poahn. Of coahse it's nawt the same as physically havin' sex with someone, but if you have imagination and a weird knack fur engineerin' crazy sexual setups, you might get pretty close to the real thing. Fur example, if you are a guy and you have access to a fleshlight, a paiyah of silicone breasts, and a VR headset, it's probably the closest you could evah get. It would be weird as all hell to own all those things, but you do you. Maybe one day virtual reality will extend past mastahbating to online poahn, and theah will be a way to connect ya central nervous system to ahnuhthah person who is nawt physically present with you. Theah might one day be microchips we stick in ah brains that communicate long distance with ah corresponding sex pahtnah's microchip. Already, theah ah some sex toys that can be controlled remotely through the Intahnet. These inventions are ideal fuh long distance relationships and could help with feelin' connected when ya nawt physically togethah. Imagine havin' the ability to make someone climax foah hundred thousand miles away? You would be like a gawd. You could give orgasms to hundreds of people across the world in real time, like if Chris Evans did a Facebook Live workout video with little to no clothes on.

We also might be able to create lifelike ahtificial intelligence whose sole purpose is to provide pleasha. Because, let's face it, what else ah we humans gonna do with sophisticated and intelligent robawts but immediately try to figure out how we can have sex with them? Theah has already been a lawt of progress made, nawt only in the field of robawtics, but in the field of sexual robawtics. Theah are automated machines out theah that can already mimic the feelin' of sex with a human. Theah is this one thing called a "Slave Driver," and boy oh boy is that thing insane lookin'. This machine kinda looks like it could be a tortcha device, but some people ah just into that kinda thing. Side note, have you evah seen a Latex Vacbed? Holy shit. It's insane! Like, if you'ah the biggest fan of BDSM and *Star Wars,* this thing is perfect fuh you. BDSM because, well, of what it was designed fur, and *Star Wars* because you'll look like that time when Han Solo was frozen in cahbonite. Look it up. I'm sorry, but also, ya welcome.

These devices could be both positive and negative. The good thing about these devices is that they fulfill an animalistic desiyah in all human bein's to feel pleasha. The bad thing about these devices is that they could make climaxing easily attainable and theahfoah rule out the need fuh the human effuht. Eventually, sexual interaction between two humans may just nawt be able to compete with these devices. Imagine havin' to compete with a robawt that is specifically designed to produce maximum sexual pleasha. SLOW YA ROLL SCIENCE AND GIVE US A BREAK! As long as love persists and we don't just staht gettin' sexual pleasha the same way we ordah fast food, then theah is hope fur us all. Unless you love fast food, then we'ah screwed.

What about aliens? Nevah thawt of that, did ya? Shoah fleshlights and vibratahs ah great and all, but what about an advanced race of aliens that invades ah planet and teaches us theah sex tips? Maybe in the futcha you'll learn how to glob a glib, or maybe even flab a flob. Maybe you've already flabbed a flob without knowing it. Some believe that aliens built the pyramids, so what if those aliens still walk among us today, and we live in some real-life *Men In Black* reality? Theah could be so many things about ah bawdies that could give us pleasha, but that we wouldn't even think to discovah until bein' tawt it by ahnuhthah alien race who has studied us fuh yeahs. Theah could even be aliens out theah that have mastahd the aht of sex and ah wise beyond all of ah yeahs as a species. Those aliens could one day touch down on Earth and tell us that we've been havin' sex all wrong. That day we might realize that *Cosmopolitan* magazine in fact does nawt know the ten best ways to plump ya lips to give maximum blow job pleasha.

Who is to say we'll even get the chance to evolve as sexual bein's? We might just have World War III and a nucleah holocaust, bringing the entiyah human race to the brink of extinction. Maybe, right now, you'ah the last known survivah in the yeah 2040, and ya tryin' to read the burnt pages of this book in the rubble of what was once a bookstoah. Hopefully, that is nawt the case. Hopefully, we have proven ahselves wrong as a species and we do in fact live long enough to exploah sex with the use of advanced technology. Whatevah technology we do create, let's just hope it doesn't end up backfirin' on us like some terrifying episode of *Black Mirror*. Imagine a world wheah it's YOU who runs out of batteries instead of ya dildo? That would be insane.

No mattah what the futcha has in stoah, whethah it be sex with silicone-covahd metal or tentacle sex in ya Donut hole, Bawstonians will always continue to have sex with love. Shoah those devices and aliens might be able to give you maximum pleasha, but humanity is about love and connection. You can do whatevah you want to do. You might love it when you light ya nipples on fiyah, strap on a dildo, and weah a printed-out mask of Mayor Manino (may he rest in peace) as ya partner weahs a printed-out mask of Sylvia Plath (may she rest in peace) and fuck each othah in front of a printed-out pictcha of John F. Kennedy (may he rest in peace). It doesn't mattah. What mattahs is that you do it all with love and that it is consensual.

One thing we can all agree on is that sex is a wondahful thing. It keeps us young, it keeps us happy, and it connects us in a way that no othah thing in life can connect us. It breaks down walls of insecurity, it brings us to a state of nirvana, and moah plainly put, it's just really freakin' awesome. Of coahse, you don't have to be frum Bawston to know that, but if you'ah frum Bawston and ya did know that then you'ah the best. You'ah nawt the best fuh knowin' all those things, you'ah the best 'cause ya frum Bawston.

Now, what ah you watin' fuh? Go out theah and have some fun. Whatevah you do, just be safe and text me when ya get home.